Comments from reviewers.

'I enthusiastically recommend this incredible story of an orphaned eleven-year-old boy who became an internationally known, highly trained and successful professional as a Pediatric Cardiologist. 'A well-traveled Way' will take you from a small village in Northern Newfoundland on an exciting journey against seemingly insurmountable odds. From a life of poverty, hardships, cultural obstacles and financial limitations, Dr. Way is a living testimony to the ability to rise above the impossible through personal faith in God and the miraculous provision of financial support from most unusual sources and people. I highly recommend this open, honest, insightful story as Dr. Way takes you through the valleys and hills, the joys and sorrows, the tragedies and triumphs on the exciting journey of 'A well-traveled Way.'

(REV. A. MORRIS RUSSELL, RETIRED PASTOR)

"From the extreme hardship of life on "The Rock" in the 1930's comes a young boy who, with God's help, is transformed into a young man with a passion for becoming a medical practitioner. This book captures the joy, trials, and tribulations of this young lad as he goes through various stages of his life's preparation traveling throughout North America learning and developing medical skills which would, in later years, equip him to become an outstanding specialist in Pediatrics Cardiology. Cliff's story is an excellent reminder to all of us as to how the Lord can intervene and take care of what we may think are life's insurmountable obstacles. Enjoy!!"

(STEVE OSWALD, FORMER CHAIRMAN, DEACONS BOARD, WEST HIGHLAND BAPTIST CHURCH, HAMILTON, ON, CANADA.)

I am delighted that Cliff has chosen to share some highlights of his life. It is a heartwarming and transparent story of how he (with strong determination, personal faith, as well as with encouragement and help along the way) rose from being an isolated orphan to a respected physician.

Rev. Dr. Grant Gordon (D.Min., Princeton Theological Seminary)

A well-traveled Way

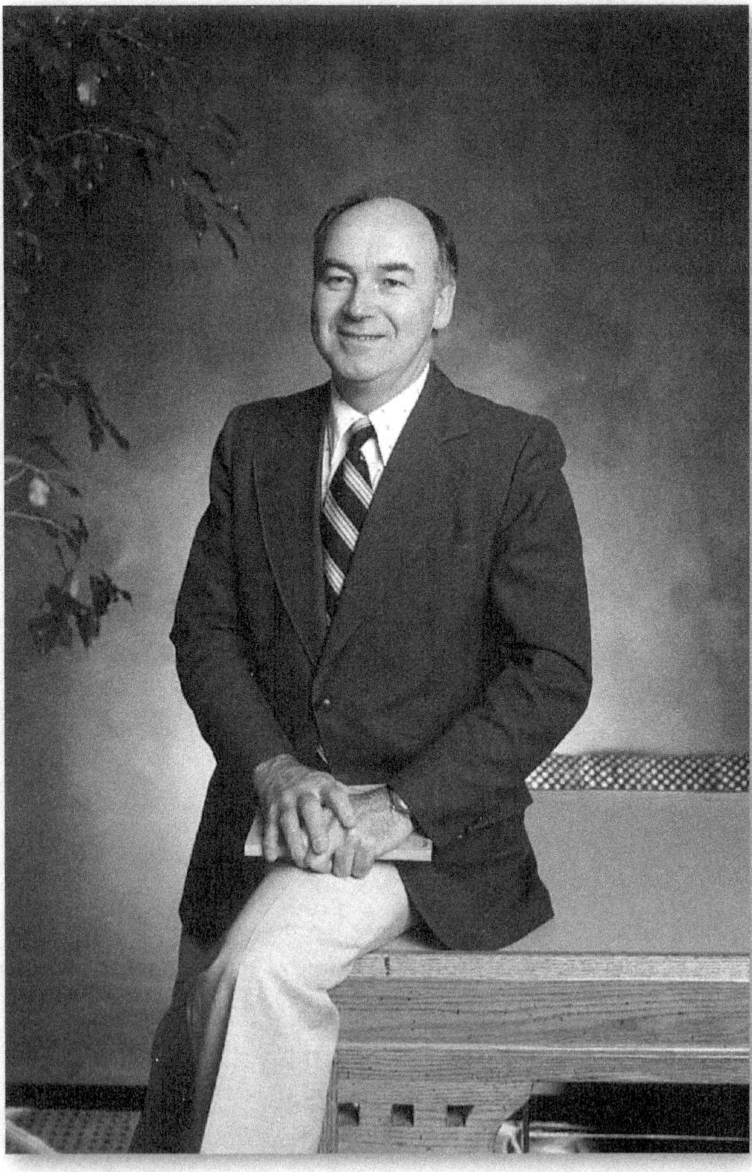

A well-traveled Way

AN AUTOBIOGRAPHY

R. Clifton Way MD
FRCPC, FACC

Emeritus Professor, Faculty of Health Sciences, McMaster University.
Founding member and former Professor, Faculty of Medicine, Memorial University of Newfoundland.
Former Instructor, Faculty of Health Sciences, University of Oregon.

A well-traveled Way
Copyright 2016, R. Clifton Way MD
All rights reserved. Reproduction of this publication, in part or whole, is not permitted, or stored in a retrieval system, or transmitted in any form or by any means – electronic, mechanical, photocopy, recording or any other – except for brief quotations in printed reviews, without the prior permission of the author.

ISBN: 1534851747
E-book ISBN: 9781534851740
(E-book available from   )
Library of Congress Control Number: 2016910301
CreateSpace Independent Publishing Platform
North Charleston, South Carolina

Catalog data available at Library and Archives Canada.
To order copies, visit:
www.awelltraveledway.com
For more information, please contact waycliff@yahoo.ca

Publisher:

Dedication

To the memory of my parents who did not have the joy of seeing their children grow to maturity.
To the memory of my stepmother and aunt, Amelia (Kean) Whalen, who loved my sister and me like her offspring and bore the burden of the death of our mother and father.
To the memory of our grandparents, Augustus and Susanna Way, who added us to their family and cared for us through our transition years from childhood to adolescence.
To the memory of Dr. Gordon Thomas, Mrs. Charles Curtis, Dr. Arthur Hill, Dr. Allan Ross, and Dr. John Darte, who made significant contributions to my professional career.
To the memory of Harold Munkittrick, who loved me as his son and 'adopted' me as such. To his wife, Peggy, who is now 97 years of age, and continues to love me as her son.
To my wife, Betty, for her love and support, her long-suffering and patience with me, and to her parents, George and Jessie Milne, who welcomed me into their family with unreserved affection.

	Introduction	xv
Chapter 1	An Unexpected Death	1
Chapter 2	My Mother	3
Chapter 3	My Early Years In Flower's Cove	8
Chapter 4	Mother's Final Year And Death	12
Chapter 5	Family Life After Mother's Death	16
Chapter 6	Father's Unexpected Death	23
Chapter 7	After Father's Death	29
Chapter 8	Living With My Way Grandparents	33
Chapter 9	Another Surprise Transition	44
Chapter 10	Life And School At St. Anthony	46
Chapter 11	Summer On The Labrador Coast	57
Chapter 12	Another Unexpected Move	62
Chapter 13	My Year At Sherbrooke High School	66
Chapter 14	Bishop's University	73
Chapter 15	Windsor Mills	80
Chapter 16	McGill Medical School	83
Chapter 17	The Medical School Experience	87
Chapter 18	A Year In Vancouver	93
Chapter 19	The Montreal Children's Hospital	96
Chapter 20	Romance And Marriage	99
Chapter 21	Our Year In St. Anthony	104

Chapter 22	The Oregon Years	115
Chapter 23	My First Days At The Janeway	123
Chapter 24	Our Life In St. John's	130
Chapter 25	Our Sabbatical Year In Toronto	140
Chapter 26	The Last Years In St. John's	144
Chapter 27	Our Years At McMaster University	148
Chapter 28	Post Retirement Years	158
Chapter 29	Family Life	162
Chapter 30	A well-traveled Way	165
Chapter 31	Final Thoughts And Commendation	166
	Appendix 1 Abbreviated Way Family Tree	169
	Appendix 2 Abbreviated Kean Family Tree	173
	Appendix 3 Abbreviated Family Tree Of Genge Families	175
	Appendix 4 Abbreviated Milne Family Tree	179
	Acknowledgements	181
	Author Biography	183

1. Map of Northern Newfoundland and South Labrador, showing road system, 1970's. xvi
2. My Mother, 1939. 3
3. My Grandparents, Roland and Amelia Kean 4
4. *White house in background was our home. Photo taken in 1942, the year after mother died, shows Father, Aunt Millie, my sister Millie and me, age 8.* 5
5. Grandfather Kean's home. One of oldest homes in Flower's Cove and original homestead of Way family. 6
6. Me at age three, winter of 1937. 8
7. My school in Flower's Cove for grades 1-9. 11
8. Grandfather Way's wharf with splitting stage on it. Note Barrels on wharf for cod liver oil. Note also fish spread to dry on flat rocks in foreground. Way family members washing fish near wharf. 19
8A. Way family homes (1960's) in background. Family members are piling fish after washing. 22
9. My father, Aubrey G. Way. 23
10. Way family photo from 1936-37. I'm the small boy lower left. Back row shows my uncles and aunts, Pierce, Max, Stewart, Abe, Pearl, Josie, Grandmother and Grandfather. Front row are Bertha, Henry and Alma. Absent is my father, Aubrey.. 30

11. Grandmother Way. 33
12. Grandfather Way in his usual work clothes. 34
13. Rev. Claude T. Mansfield. 44
14. Sir Wilfred T. Grenfell, 1865-1940. 46
15. St. Anthony Orphanage. 50
16. Me, fall of 1947 at gate of Brown Cottage. Note my hair perm is still present from my aunties in Flower's Cove. 52
17. Original Grenfell School. Scripture on wall states "All thy children shall be taught of the Lord, and great shall be the peace of thy children." 53
18. Wrecked schooner in Labrador. Boat in distance is Maraval. 58
19. Dr. Paddon with patient in tent. 60
20. Mrs. Charles Curtis 62
21. Dr. Arthur C. Hill. 67
22. Mr. and Mrs. Clem Best. 68
23. Harold and Peggy Munkittrick, June 1988. 73
24. Visiting with my sister, Summer 1952. 78
25. Graduation photo, Bishop's University, 1953. 79
26. Me, as Deck Steward. 85
27. With Peggy Munkittrick and Aunt Selina (Kean) Headge, Montreal, Spring 1958. 89
28. As MGH Interne and Resident, 1958-60. 90
29. Betty as student nurse. 92
30. Bert and Marion McGee and three of their children. A fourth arrived later. 94
31. After the ceremony, December 28, 1963 102
32. Dr. Gordon W. Thomas. 108
33. Betty's parents, Jessie and George Milne 110
34. The Janeway as I knew it. 122
35. Dr. C. J. Joy. 127
36. Dr. J. M. Darte 131

37. My car in the river. March 1981, near Antigonish, NS. 151
38. McMaster ID photo, March 1981 152
39. Family gathering, Thanksgiving 2010. Adults, Steven and Liz, Caroline, Susan and Ian, Cliff and Betty, Debbie and Gregory. Grandchildren, Sarah and Seth (Susan), Lucas and Thomas (Gregory), Eleanor and Veronica (Steven). 163

Introduction

FATHER'S DAY 1993, CAME AND went without much fanfare. I had entered my 60th year and, for the first time I realized that time was passing, and I should make a record of my life story. Many of you will read this account because you are part of the Way or Kean family with roots in Newfoundland. Some will read it because you recognize the name from my time as a medical practitioner, university teacher, or my involvement in church affairs. But most of you will know little about my roots, my traumatic childhood and teenage struggles, and my career as a pediatric cardiologist. This record is made primarily for my children and grandchildren with the aim of helping them understand themselves more fully through the story of their Father and Grandfather. It is also intended to document some of the early history of the Janeway Child Health Centre in St. John's, Newfoundland, and the development of Pediatric Cardiology at McMaster University in Hamilton, both of which were significant parts of my career.

To my friends, colleagues, former patients, and their parents, I hope and pray that my story might be a rewarding read and personal blessing.

I have been working on this project for over twenty years, since 1993, when I first sat at my computer and began to detail my family tree. I have tried to record relevant parts of family history, the crises of my childhood and adolescence, and my education and career as a pediatric cardiologist. I am not a professional author, and this has been a tough job so I hope my story will be of interest to a larger audience as well as the four generations that have been added to my family since I was born. Whatever the consequences, my hope and prayer are that it will be a useful and rewarding read.

May God bless you all as you follow me through my well-traveled way.

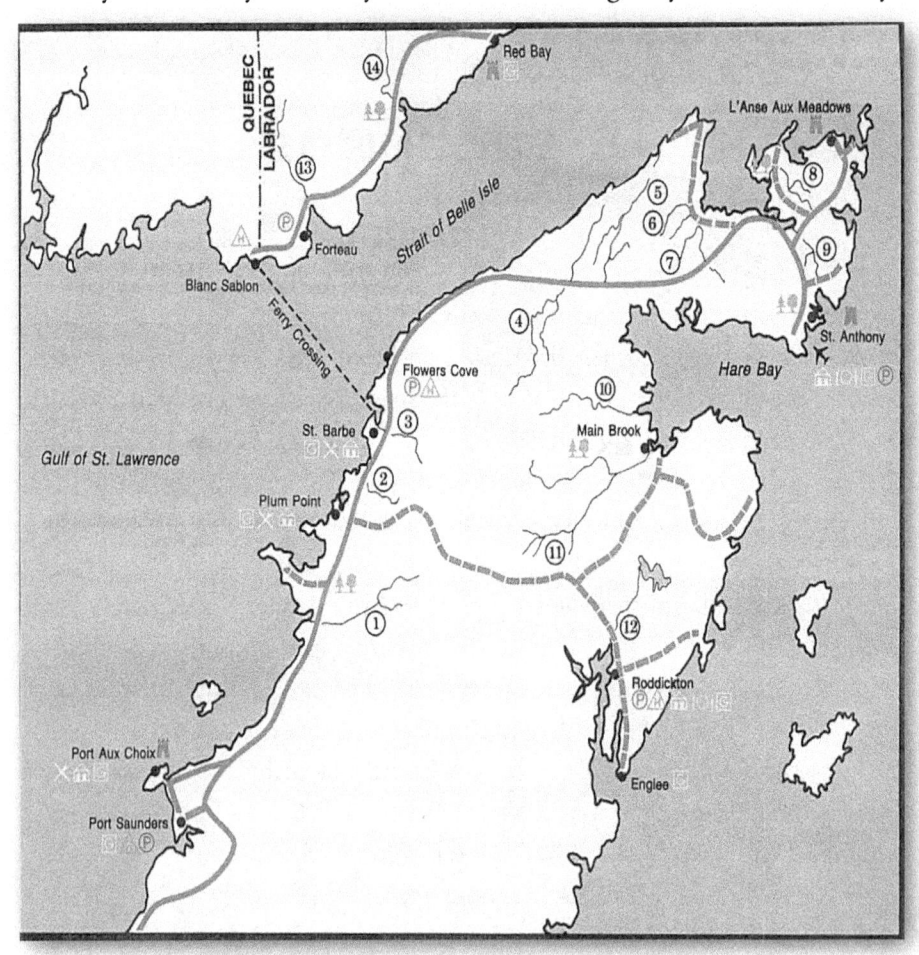

1. Map of Northern Newfoundland and South Labrador, showing road system, 1970's.

CHAPTER 1

An Unexpected Death

IT WAS NOVEMBER 1941, AND winter was arriving in Flower's Cove, a fishing community near the tip of the great northern peninsula in Newfoundland. Its 250 residents were bedding down for winter and Christmas celebrations. Except.... for one family.

The Way family, on the south side of the harbor, was worried about the status of Caroline, wife of Aubrey. She had been re-admitted to the Grenfell Mission Hospital at St. Anthony, some 100 kilometers to the northeast, which serviced the expansive region of Northern Newfoundland and Labrador. "Carrie," as she was known, was there previously, in April, when a surgeon removed a tumor from her thigh which proved to be non-malignant. After spending a good summer helping with the fish, she was back there again. Her two small children, affectionately called 'Cliffy' and 'Millie', were at home in the care of their Aunt Millie, Carrie's youngest sister, who was still recovering from tuberculosis. Aubrey was working twenty miles away in the logging camps of Bowater Company, and trying to earn enough to provide for his family. Three weeks had gone by with no news from the hospital, but people were trusting of their doctors and always considered that 'no news was good news.' The weather was in transition with winter coming, so few people were traveling at that time of year. No telephone service was available, and people used the telegraph in the Post Office primarily for emergency messages. The family listened to radio broadcasts by Gerald S. Doyle, which included daily news about the patients at the hospital – who had surgery, who was doing well, and who was ready for home. Carrie's status was unmentioned, but on November 26th a telegraph message arrived. Carrie had died.

Carrie was my mother. I was seven years old, and my sister was two.

CHAPTER 2

My Mother

Caroline (Kean) Way, [1912 -1941]

Mother was the oldest daughter of Roland and Amelia Kean. Roland was born and raised in Pool's Island, on the central east coast of Newfoundland, and came north at age nineteen to teach school at Deadman's Cove, just a few kilometers south of Flower's Cove. It was there he fell in love with Amelia Genge. She was one of his pupils but only three years younger and smashingly beautiful. They married in December 1909, when Roland was twenty-one and lived in Deadman's Cove for the next three years before building a home in Flower's Cove and moving there permanently. In 1922 they sold their large new home to Henry Genge, one of the local merchants, and bought a smaller old house in the center of town that was the original homestead of the Way family.

2. My Mother, 1939.

My grandfather Kean was a brilliant man. He was from a large family famous for fishing, seal hunting, politics, and medicine, at the beginning of the twentieth century in Newfoundland. He quickly gained prominence in Flower's Cove because of his education and leadership skills. He supported Cannon J. T. Richards in building the new Anglican Church in the community. He was a friend of Dr. Wilfred T. Grenfell, who constructed a nursing station in 1919 as part of establishing medical services in the region. Grandfather was appointed as Government Land Surveyor for the area and later served as manager of the Co-operative Society of Fishermen, which began in 1920 under the guidance of Dr. Grenfell.

3. My Grandparents, Roland and Amelia Kean

By the time Carrie was a young adult, her father was well established and prospering economically. Unfortunately, the depression of 1930-33 affected his economic status, and the children were required to seek employment at an early age rather than higher education.

Roland and Amelia had six children. The oldest and only son was Cecil. Carrie was the second born followed by four sisters, Stella, Marjorie, Selina, and Amelia.

Cecil completed school and moved away from home. He went to work with Bowater Paper Company – owners of a paper mill at Corner Brook, and the logging camps on the northern peninsula. Most of the young men in Flower's Cove, including my father and his brothers, worked some time in the logging camps, especially during the winter months.

The young ladies worked at home as domestics, moved away for training as nursing aids or teachers, or became clerks in one of the dry goods stores in the community. Flower's Cove had four stores, all operated by members of the Genge family – three were brothers of Carrie's mother, and one was a cousin.

When Carrie completed high school, she began work as a clerk in the dry goods business of Henry Genge, the cousin, located next door to her home. She was under considerable stress because of her mother's prolonged depression following each pregnancy, which meant she was expected to do housekeeping as well as her job at the store. The economic depression also required Stella to seek work to bring in some income. As a result, the next oldest sister, Marjorie, who was only thirteen, had to function now as the housekeeper. Selina (eleven) and Amelia (nine) were still attending school.

The family pressures increased when their mother contracted tuberculosis and died unexpectedly in the summer of 1930.

The job at the store was pleasant and brought Carrie into contact with many people from the community and surrounding area. It also placed her into contact with the store's handyman who brought salt pork, sugar, flour, and molasses from the warehouse for customers as needed. The handyman, Aubrey Way, was only seventeen - four years younger than she was - but mature for his age and very handsome. Romance soon developed which, as was common in the area, led to premature intimacy and pregnancy. Aubrey felt compelled to offer marriage and Carrie accepted, so they were married just before Christmas in 1933. They were invited to share an old clapboard house across the harbor, owned by Aubrey's Aunt Moriah, who was widowed six years previous, and felt she needed a man to help fetch wood and water and do repairs. Aubrey and Carrie were made welcome by Aunt Moriah and her daughter, Beatrice.

The house had a small windowless porch area for storage of wood and boots. The living area had a large living room with a wood burning stove, homemade wooden table and chairs, a dish cupboard and kitchen work area. Two of the outside walls

4. White house in background was our home. Photo taken in 1942, the year after mother died, shows Father, Aunt Millie, my sister Millie and me, age 8.

contained a small window with four single panes of glass. A long wide wooden bench along one wall completed the sparse furnishings and served as an extra seat or daybed as needed. A wall behind the kitchen stove created a long narrow room accessed through a door to the left of the stove. This room was unfurnished and used for special occasions only.

The bedrooms were upstairs and reached through an enclosed corner stairway which had a sharp turn in it. Upstairs, the ceiling was low on the sides but high enough for standing in the center because of the peaked roof structure. Small windows in the hall at the top of the stairwell and in each of the three bedrooms helped give a feeling of warmth to the flowery wallpaper and white painted ceiling. The only source of heat was the tin stovepipe which came up from the kitchen stove into the hallway. There was no running water or plumbing but in an alcove of the hall, there was a small wooden stand, with mirror and lace cloth, containing a large porcelain basin and water jug. Each bedroom had a chamber pot, commonly known as a 'come-under-me-quick,' for use in urinary or other emergencies.

Carrie was very soft hearted and not aggressive. She adjusted well to the Way family environment and related well to Aunt Moriah and Aubrey's family, who lived next door. Her pregnancy was evident soon after the marriage, and she delivered a son in the early morning of April 10th, 1934. The birth occurred at her father's home, across the harbor, under the supervision of the nurse from the Grenfell Mission

5. Grandfather Kean's home. One of oldest homes in Flower's Cove and original homestead of Way family.

station. The child was given the name Roland Clifton Kean Way, borrowing heavily from her father's name (Harold Clifton Roland Kean). That child was me.

CHAPTER 3

My Early Years In Flower's Cove

(1934 -1947)

THE WORLD WAS AT PEACE and had been that way for fifteen years when I was born in 1934. There were hard times in spite of the peace and recovery from war, especially in Northern Newfoundland. The great depression was coming to an end but the overture to the Second World War was about to begin. The Colony of Newfoundland had become self-governing in 1855, twelve years before Canadian Confederation, but it was now bankrupt. It had lost thousands of young men in the First World War. The resultant war debt and pension responsibilities, together with the cost of operating the trans-island railway, had emptied its treasury. The British Crown appointed a Commission to govern the island's affairs in February 1934.

Cliff as small boy. Note Grandfather's old store where he built boats.

6. Me at age three, winter of 1937.

The economic lifeline in Flower's Cove was fishing, and it had floundered for some years leaving families victims of the 'truck' system where the local merchant extended credit during the winter months in exchange for buying the fish catch, at his price, the following summer. The Ways were a fishing family and felt the economic pinch of several poor fishing seasons. Fortunately, the family did not lose any of its young men during the war, so they worked at the logging camps in nearby Hawke's Bay and Main Brook to provide income during the winter months.

My life as an infant and small child was very typical for an outport boy. From an early age, I was curious and inquisitive. I talked and walked at the normal age and soon began to 'motor' the short distance between our home and grandmother's house. We were coping financially as my father kept working extra time at several jobs in the logging industry and did not participate in the fishery. Mother worked hard in the home with Aunt Moriah and Beatrice, but father's extended absences meant she depended on his younger brothers for help with the heavier aspects of providing firewood and water when needed. We were excited as a family when my brother, Baxter, arrived shortly after my second birthday but saddened by his death from pneumonia two years later. I have little recollection of this, but I do remember he was placed in a small white casket on a table in the long room behind the kitchen stove. I have no recollection of how I felt about losing my little brother, but it was a sad time for all of us. My sister Amelia, 'Millie' as she is known, was born five years after me and completed our family.

A brief family crisis arose when I was about four and a half years of age. Aunt Moriah and my mother had a falling out. I do not know the issue but, Aunt Moriah and Beatrice decided to move across the Strait of Belle Isle to Labrador, to live with her other daughter. The old house was now ours, and I am not sure if my father paid something to take possession, or it was a gift to him. However, I was old enough to share the tension of the family quarrel and the anxiety that was present as regard our remaining in the house.

From an early age, I was curious and inquisitive. My curiosity sometimes got me into trouble. When I was about three years old, and wandering next door to visit grandmother, I tried to befriend a ram that was feeding in the field. He didn't take kindly to my approaches and started to attack me. Fortunately, grandmother was watching and rushed to my rescue before he did any damage.

After starting school, I remember being quarantined at home for such childhood illnesses as scarlet fever, chicken pox, measles, and mumps. I also endured times of quarantine to deal with scabies and head lice brought home from school. I do not remember any conversations, special times, events, or unpleasant incidents that I experienced during my preschool years. I never got to know my father well, or feel close to him, because of his prolonged absences at work, and when he was home, his social activity was centered on visiting with the men who were his circle of friends rather than spending family time with me, my sister and mother.

I was not ready for separation from mom when I started school at four and a half years of age, but she dragged me the full mile and made sure the teacher had a firm hold of my hand before letting go. My father's youngest sisters (Alma and Bertha) were attending school with me, and they helped me settle when I arrived and took me home safely at the end of the school day. After a short time, I thought it was fun to walk home with them and be in their company.

My curiosity kept me going and there were more books to explore at school than there were at home. Grandmother Way once commented that 'Cliffy would pick the eyes out of your head if you would let him.' I explored and examined things with moving parts and wanted to learn to spell words and read. Books were fascinating, and I wanted to know about the pictures and what the words were saying. A few radio stations were available in our area, and I loved to listen to the news, music, and comedy broadcasts. Grandfather had the only radio and his house had lots of uncles and aunts to give me attention. The house next door to Grandfather's contained several cousins who were my playmates. I loved to play Chinese checkers, marbles, and card games with family members.

My formal education began in the one-room school of the United (Methodist) Church in Flower's Cove. There were three schools in the small community, because of the denominational system, serving a school population of about one hundred. In our school, the teacher was also the Church leader and conducted worship services on Sunday. School days began with a half hour of religious exercises consisting of reading of scripture, recitation, singing of choruses, and prayer. Before long I had memorized many of the choruses and loved to participate in singing duets with Mary Diamond. Mary and I were paired together often in our school years, up to grade nine, and it is fair to say that if I had grown up at home, we might have become life partners.

7. My school in Flower's Cove for grades 1-9.

CHAPTER 4

Mother's Final Year And Death

MY MOTHER'S LIFE, FROM THE time of my birth through to attendance at school, was stable and healthy. She was a hard worker, of necessity, as father worked in the lumber camps during the winter months and she was left alone to care for the home for several weeks at a time. I was not the easiest child to care for without having a dad around. My inquisitive nature required constant monitoring because of a tendency to explore and pick apart anything within my vision and reach. When I was outdoors, I needed watching because of a tendency to get too friendly with animals.

I had just turned seven in April 1941 when my mother became ill with a growth on her thigh. The nurse in Flower's Cove sent her to St. Anthony for admission to the Grenfell Mission Hospital. Mother's youngest sister, Aunt Millie, came to care for us while she was away.

Winter conditions still existed in April, so mother traveled the 100 kilometers overland wrapped warmly in a coach box lashed to a komatik (sled) and pulled by a team of dogs. The tumor was removed and analyzed. It appeared benign, and she recovered well. She was discharged a month later and returned home by boat. She was healthy for about eight months and participated fully in family life, including splitting, curing, washing and drying fish during the spring and summer months. Then tragedy struck without much warning.

In late October, mother became ill again, this time with progressive abdominal swelling and she was transported by boat to the hospital at St. Anthony. Aunt Millie came again as our caretaker. I was aware of what was happening, but my mother had been ill before and came back well after a time, so I was not unduly worried. My father was away in the lumber camps and not aware that mother had become ill. There were no quick means of communication at the time, and the family did not appreciate the serious nature of her illness. Twenty-five years later, when I became a staff doctor at the hospital, I had access to her medical records and here is what they showed.

She was admitted to the hospital on November 1 and appeared very ill, having lost considerable weight, despite a progressively distending abdomen. On November 6 she was taken to the operating room for exploratory surgery. The surgeon made a small incision in her abdomen, and an enormous amount of 'foul smelling pus' greeted him. He saw what he recognized as tubercles (deposits of tuberculosis) studded over the surface of her bowel. The diagnosis of advanced tuberculous peritonitis was clear. At the time, there was no drug treatment known for tuberculosis – that did not happen until after 1945. The situation was hopeless, and she died on the morning of November 26.

Back in Flower's Cove, a telegram arrived to inform the family she had died. Arrangements had to be made to have her returned for burial. As a family, we were all stricken with grief and panic, not only about the future but also about the immediate arrangements that had to be made for our care and for getting her home for burial. Father was contacted and brought home, and this took a couple of days. The owner of the best dog team in town volunteered himself and his dogs to go to the lumber camp and bring father home.

The season was in transition between fall and winter. Small boat travel was very dangerous this late in the year and dog team travel could be difficult with uncertain snow and ice conditions. Her transport was managed by dog team as there had been a snowfall. Some of the transfer was by boat across brooks where no bridge existed. In one area a large stream had to be crossed, and the casket lashed to a komatik (dogsled), was floated across while the dog team and drivers crossed by boat.

My Mother had been dead for over a week when her remains arrived home. I remember seeing her after she arrived. The casket was resting on a table in the long narrow room behind the stove – the room not used for normal living. It had been used once previously when my baby brother died and was placed there in his little white casket.

Mother's coffin was prepared at the Grenfell Mission machine shop in St. Anthony. The outside had a nice purple covering and chrome handles while the inside had a white satin lining. She had a dark yellowish brown color and looked very emaciated. Later, I learned her color was due to jaundice (produced by liver failure) in her final days. I can't recall my feelings at seeing her in this way except that I was numb and blocked out much of the details forever from my memory. My sister was only two and could not comprehend the significance of what was happening. Aunt Millie did her best to shield her personal grief, and comfort and distract us even as she saw no escape from continuing indefinitely as our caregiver and homemaker.

Digging a grave in Flower's Cove in November was not as difficult as in January or February as the ground had not yet frozen to its full depth, but it was still a demanding job for several men. On a cold December day, my mother was laid to rest, and we all came back to the old house feeling numb and empty. Father was still bewildered, wondering how he could cope with returning to the logging camps to earn a few dollars to feed us while relying on Aunt Millie to continue as our caregiver, in winter conditions, even as she recovered from tuberculosis. Father's younger brothers willingly volunteered to continue supporting Aunt Millie so that he could return to his work at the lumber camps.

Only one memento remains from my mother. Grandmother Way kept a small jar labeled 'Freckle Cream' which came from her personal things. Mother had very prominent freckles on her face and arms and tried the cream as a removal remedy. After I had graduated in medicine, Grandmother gave me that jar, and I have kept it to pass on to one of my children. Recently, I searched the internet and discovered that Stillman's Freckle Cream is still available, some seventy-five years later, in a jar that looks unchanged.

CHAPTER 5

Family Life After Mother's Death

THE NEWS OF MOTHER'S DEATH was a devastating shock to the Way and Kean families and the residents of Flower's Cove and surrounding communities. Aunt Millie had been our caregiver for about a month before mother died. She was eighteen when she came to care for us and had been 'resting' for the previous year, because of tuberculosis, and was considered stable, yet fragile.

My sister and I were very comfortable with Aunt Millie and, even though we missed our mother, we settled back into as normal a family life as possible. Aunt Millie also felt lonely for our mom, and we often had crying sessions together where we comforted each other. She must have felt trapped in the situation as father saw no recourse but to rely on her to care for us while he went back to the lumber camps to earn some income.

Grandmother Way and the family comforted us and helped in any way they could. I went back to school accompanied by Aunt alma and Aunt Bertha. My sister, being only two, was kept at home. Father went back to the lumber camps and returned home for a few days every three or four weeks. He came home for Christmas week, 1941, just a month after mother died. We were all sorrowful and subdued as a family, and there was little to celebrate. We had a few simple gifts for Christmas, but there was nothing to relieve our sadness. I wore a black armband in mourning

A well-traveled Way

for nearly a year, as was the custom then, and all family members did the same.

The winter months were frigid and stressful. We had a woodpile outside, but the wood was green and wet and required cutting into junks for burning. I was not strong enough to saw the wood and, with father away; my teenage uncles helped cut firewood and bring it into the porch to be kept dry. They were good about this generally but, like all teenagers, they sometimes let us down, and an older uncle would come to our rescue. Water had to be brought in buckets from the nearby pond and, although I helped with that chore in summer, in winter it was necessary to cut through the ice, and this required the strength of a teenager or adult.

It was wartime and supplies, as well as money, were in short supply. Father managed to bring home enough funds to keep us in necessities, but there was no reserve for a rainy day. When spring came, we began to see convoys and warships passing through the Strait of Belle Isle. German submarines were present, and rumors abounded that spies were around. U-boats followed some convoys and some ships, after being attacked, ran aground to save their cargo from total loss. At such times, cargo salvage provided sugar, flour, and other food items which were rationed and in short supply. Even though the food was wet, or tainted with the taste of fuel oil, it was appreciated. We had to observe a blackout at night because of the situation.

When summer came, and school was out, I was able to get outside and play. As an eight-year-old, I had some buddies living nearby. Chesley ('Ches') was my closest friend, and we played at his house with several of his younger siblings. Abe lived down the road, and he often joined us for outdoor games. In winter, we built snowmen or went sledding down the slopes or snowdrifts. Sometimes we amused ourselves with snowball fights. A few of us had old fashioned clamp-on skates which we attached to boots and used on the frozen ponds.

One of our favorite activities in summer was to play 'copy house' where we would go into the nearby bush and set up a play house with dishes, make-believe chairs and table, a stove, and even some beds. The girls were very imaginative in creating these places while the boys were sometimes mean-spirited in pulling apart what they had constructed. Part of the activity sometimes involved pretending we were mother and father and family within the home situation. I was the shy one in our gang as regards to role playing and acting out father or husband roles. The other boys were 'men of the world' at a much earlier age than I. They brought to our circle the first knowledge of 'the birds and the bees'. Before the age of ten, I was aware of sexual things, even before my body was awakening in this area. My teenage uncles were all 'courting', and I knew the implications of that activity. However, while I was very curious, some of the secret things that gang members spoke about or wanted to act out were still repulsive to me.

At other times, as boys, we played with sailboats in the small pond near our house or, wearing our knee high rubber boots, we waded in the saltwater ponds at low tide to catch minnows and crabs. I was excited to receive my first pair of knee-high rubber boots. Naturally, I had to test them and, as usually happened, I went out too far and got them filled with water. A year or so later I was equally excited to graduate to thigh high rubber boots and wade out deeper to catch trout with a fishing pole or catch salmon and arctic char by the tail as they lay beside the bank or rocks in the nearby brook.

When I reached ten, I was allowed to accompany the men in the fishing boat and participate in hauling the cod trap and bringing the fish to land. Grandfather had an assigned trap 'berth' some distance outside the harbor and near the shore of a small barren island. Our catch often included salmon, lobsters, halibut, and small shark fish, which we called dogfish because they were used to feed the dogs. Once in a while, we were surprised by a large catch which filled the boat, and we had to motor home carefully to avoid submersion. Then we spent several hours splitting and salting the fish and storing it in a shed to be cured for several weeks. I participated by lifting the fish from the wharf to the splitting table or, using a prong, throwing the fish from the boat onto the pier.

A well-traveled Way

The splitting table was a special place. It was set up on the wharf in a rough wooden shelter to protect the men and women from the wind and sun. An assembly line of attendants started with someone picking up the fish from the wharf and placing them on the table. A table attendant then partially severed the head and split open the fish belly from neck to tail. The fish slid to a second attendant who removed the liver and dropped it, through a hole in the table, into a barrel. A third attendant removed the innards, completed severing the head, and directed the head and guts via a chute into the water where scavenger fish were awaiting eagerly. The fourth attendant was the splitter, an individual adept at using a curved knife, who removed the sound bone (spinal vertebrae), directing it into the water while sliding the split fish into a waiting wheelbarrow. The liver was allowed to cure and render into oil. The split fish were wheeled to a nearby shed, salted, and placed in square piles (salt bulk) for curing. After several weeks the curing process was complete and, watching for a sunny day, the fish were taken and washed with mops in a tidal pond at the water's edge, then spread out to dry on a large area of flat rocks we were fortunate to have for this purpose. I helped spread fish on the rocks, pick them up at the end of the day and pile them in a dry place. This process occurred daily, weather permitting until the fish was ready for market. The final step was to take

8. Grandfather Way's wharf with splitting stage on it. Note Barrels on wharf for cod liver oil. Note also fish spread to dry on flat rocks in foreground. Way family members washing fish near wharf.

the dried fish across the harbor by boat where it was weighed and sold to the local merchant who had provided, on credit, the living necessities for the previous winter plus whatever gear was needed. Hopefully, there would be a few dollars available for 'luxuries' or as credit towards the needs for next year. This trip, to sell the fish, was always exciting for me as I got to spend a day riding in the boat and visiting the stores. The men oversaw the weighing and inspection of our catch and completed the business of paying for the credit received in the past year and receiving any cash or credit due for the next year. I always had a family member working as a clerk in one of the stores, and the owners were all relatives so that candy or bubble gum treats were usual.

The first six months of 1942 passed quickly and, at home, we were coping well with the loss of mother and Aunt Millie soon became accepted as her replacement. Father kept going off to work in the lumber woods for several weeks at a time followed by short stints at home to visit with us. I went back to school after a happy summer and continued to do well academically but remained small physically. By late fall, I was aware that romance was developing between my father and Aunt Millie. I noted that they were no longer sleeping in separate rooms and, as I lay contemplating what I had learned from the gang, the rhythmic creaking of the bed in father's room came to make sense. They were married in April 1943 and had a happy relationship for the next two years until father's untimely death. No children resulted from their marriage. Naturally, my curiosity about sexual things was greatly aroused by this and, even though I never shared what was happening at home, information from the gang enhanced my understanding during the subsequent years.

I continued to advance in academics at school so that by age ten I was doing the work of grade six and, just after my thirteenth birthday, I wrote grade nine exams. As I entered my middle school years our teacher was Rev. Claude Mansfield. He was a bachelor and boarded with Aunt Rachel

(Way) Rose, widowed daughter of the original John Way in Flower's Cove. Rev. Mansfield was a good teacher, and disciplinarian, considering he had pupils from beginners to grade nine. In those years, many children, in Flower's Cove, did not remain in school beyond age fifteen. The girls tended to start into domestic or clerical work by that age, and many were married by age eighteen. Many boys lost interest as teens and wanted to earn money, so they could build a home and marry, rather than continue the uncertain path to grade eleven and higher education. There were few role models in the community to encourage them to complete their schooling, and there was no compulsion to do so.

I was small and not athletic but enjoyed participation in soccer. The school had limited athletic facilities with no gym or organized physical program, and no soccer field or playground. I got into mischief with the boys in a typical normal way. There were some bushes on the edge of the school grounds and one day we decided we would try smoking. We had no cigarettes, but we fashioned some brown wrapping paper and dried leaves into a reasonable resemblance. We lit one end with a match and, in turn, 'took a draw'. There was lots of acrid smoke which produced a sickening taste and generated spasms of choking, coughing and red eyes. Some girls squealed on us and after recess the teacher lined us up in front of his desk, quizzed us, and proceeded to administer the belt to our hands. Getting 'the strap' was an unusual happening for me as I was considered the teacher's pet and 'goodie-good' student. That was the end of my career as a smoker!

As I became a pre-teenager I was also exposed to alcohol since home brew, 'Moonshine', was commonly prepared by my uncles in preparation for holidays, weddings, and other celebration events - 'times' as we called these gatherings - when dancing, eating, drinking and socializing in other ways took place. I remember tasting the dregs in empty bottles, like curious boys will do, but I never liked the taste. As the war ended my uncles had access to beer and, again, I found the taste terrible and lost any desire to patronize the beer outlets.

8A. Way family homes (1960's) in background. Family members are piling fish after washing.

CHAPTER 6

Father's Unexpected Death

(May 1945)

THROUGHOUT 1944, THE WORLD WAS unsettled and the future uncertain. World War II still raged in Europe, and the outcome was unclear. Germany's offense was in check, but the fighting remained intense and casualties were high. Father left his job in the lumber camps at Hawke's Bay, just 30 kilometers from home, and took a war effort job as a carpenter in Gander, some 600 kilometers away. The distance from home was great, and travel in winter was difficult, but there was an urgency to complete the Gander Airport. The airport was an essential support for transatlantic flight and defense of the northeast coast of North America. It was one of several war projects in Newfoundland, paid for by the United States, designed to prevent the European conflict from extending across the Atlantic.

9. My father, Aubrey G. Way.

As Christmas approached my sister and me were excited that Dad would be home for the holidays, and we would be complete as a family for a few weeks. He had been away for three months, and winter had arrived to increase our problems with getting water and firewood. I was nearly eleven, and my sister was six. Mother's death was three years behind us, and we had recovered from her loss. Aunt Millie was a wonderful stepmother. She and father were happy together, and we were happy in her care. Her health had remained stable through all the stress she endured, and she loved us as though we were her children. The distance father had to travel to and from work was a problem, especially once winter came, and his prolonged absences made life stressful for us. We were all lonely. Like all of the Way family, we depended on Uncle Ike Genge to extend us credit for food. We also needed the support of our teenage uncle's to cut firewood, bring water from the pond, and shovel snow drifts from the entrance when needed.

Father arrived home after a week of traveling and participated in Mummering. This Christmas-time tradition existed in Newfoundland and Labrador and parts of Ireland. Groups went from house to house in disguise, and father was a master at disguise as he was not home often and had become a relative stranger in town. Some visits led to drinking of home brew (moonshine), music, singing, and dancing. Father could play the mouth organ and accordion and often supplied the music during visits – which usually unmasked any disguise.

He was making better wages in Gander so that we could afford a few extra things for Christmas. In those years, my gifts would include some candy, an apple or orange, a toy, and an item of clothing such as a shirt, new pants, jacket, or rubber boots. It was wartime, so shopping choices were limited and mail orders from Eaton's catalog, or the Royal Stores in St. John's, could be lost in transit by misadventure such as a torpedoed boat or some other mishap.

Our Christmas season did not end until January 6 of the New Year, recognized in the Christian Orthodox calendar as 'Old Christmas.' The men in the community participated in a final bash on that day. My father took part in the partying and came home around midnight. He was somewhat drunk but found his way, in the darkness, across the harbor ice and arrived home safely. On rounding the house, a patch of ice caused him to slip and hit his head on the corner of the building. After recovering his senses, he went to bed but woke in the morning with an intense headache and a bruised and swollen forehead. After a day or so, he felt well enough to begin the trip back to Gander, walking and hitchhiking rides by dog team and finding shelter and food in the small communities along the 300-kilometer route to Deer Lake. It was tough going and it took a week, following which he took the train another 300 kilometers to Gander. He returned to work and managed to cope with a persistent headache for the next few weeks. As winter wore on in the New Year, 1945, Newfoundland remained deeply involved in the war in Europe and, as spring approached, fears of a North Atlantic invasion were present even though allied landings in Europe were beginning to encircle and contain Germany's aggression. Completion of the Gander Airport was still considered essential.

In March father's headaches became worse and he developed nausea and vomiting which progressed in severity and forced him to return home from Gander. The return trip was very arduous, and he had to hitch rides from Deer Lake with the mail carriers on their dog teams as there were no other means of travel except to walk using snowshoes. He was very ill during this unpleasant trip, and he fell off the dogsled several times during the final part of the journey.

He arrived home safely and went for an assessment at the Grenfell Mission Station in Flower's Cove. The nurse referred him to the hospital at St. Anthony where a further examination led to admission on April 16th, one week after my 11th Birthday. My later access to his medical records provided details of his final illness.

A Dr. Miller examined him carefully. Looking back on this now, I am better able to understand father's condition and describe what followed. The doctor detected some nonspecific neurologic signs - mild increase in reflexes and possible tremor but no signs to indicate one side of his brain was affected which would have helped with localization of any problem. Next day a lumbar puncture (cerebrospinal fluid [CSF] tap via a needle inserted between the lower back vertebrae) revealed a marked elevation in the fluid pressure, confirming there was a problem blocking the normal flow of fluid around the brain. The findings were helpful, indicating the problem could be a blood clot on the brain surface (subdural hematoma) or a brain tumor distorting and blocking the normal fluid flow channels around and within the brain and spinal column. The fluid was clear and normal-looking, and analysis of its contents showed no abnormality. There was no worry about infection or fresh bleeding inside his head. The history of head injury made the doctor think of a probable subdural hematoma, and he noted that the pressure fell to normal with the removal of spinal fluid. Father felt better following this procedure but remained in the hospital for observation. After a week his symptoms returned. Skull X-rays revealed no fracture. A repeat lumbar puncture showed a return of the elevated pressure which was again reduced by the removal of some fluid, with relief of symptoms.

However, within a couple of days symptoms were back and another lumbar puncture was necessary, with identical findings and relief. After a further three days, symptoms came back and were worse. On May 7 it was decided that exploratory surgery was necessary. Before beginning surgery, another lumbar puncture confirmed very high pressure was again present. Under anesthesia, a burr hole drilled in the right temple area of his skull revealed no blood clot or abnormality. Downward enlargement of the hole continued to reveal normal findings. This same procedure and sequence was repeated on the left temple and, again, everything appeared normal. Father was still under anesthesia.

The doctors decided to insert air into the fluid-filled spaces (ventricles) of his brain and take X-ray photos to try and identify if there was a blockage in the flow of fluid out of these spaces. This new procedure, called a pneumoencephalogram, was used only at university centers in the 1940's - in places like Montreal and Boston. My father may have been the first ever to have it done in Newfoundland. After the air insertion, the burr holes were sealed, and father was moved, still under anesthesia, from the operating room down one floor to the X-ray department. The x-rays failed to identify any abnormality, particularly evidence of fluid blockage, tumor, or shifts in brain structure. The smaller brain ventricles were not visible as no air had entered them.

Despite undergoing this horrendous day-long ordeal, father remained in stable condition, awoke from anesthesia, and talked to the nurses. He was taken back to continue recovery and appeared to be doing well through the late afternoon. At one point he again awoke from his sedated state and spoke to the nurse. But, at 7:25 pm, while a nurse was watching him, he suddenly gasped, stopped breathing and became cyanotic (blue). Dr. Miller was nearby and examined him immediately to find his heart had stopped. Emergency measures failed to resuscitate him. At post-mortem, a small tumor was found at the base of his brain which obstructed the flow of fluid. There was no evidence of any blood clot from the injury in January.

The next day, May 8th, 1945, was an important date in world history. It was VE (Victory in Europe) Day. The family in Flower's Cove was gathered at Grandfather Way's home to listen to the radio and hear the news from Europe. Winston Churchill was making his famous speech when a courier arrived with a telegram from the Post Office across the harbor. Someone opened the envelope and screeched in grief as they conveyed the news to us that my father was dead. I was present at the family gathering and shared in the numbing grief expressed by all of us as we tried to come to terms with the new reality.

Aunt Millie was not present at the family gathering so Uncle Max, one of my father's brothers, accompanied me back to our house to break the news to her. It was a devastating time for her, and for us, as we tried to regain our composure from the shock and think about the future. Our cousin, Grant, rushed on foot to the other side of the harbor to take the news to Grandfather Kean and his family.

The whole family supported us as, together, we made plans for father's return. Again, house curtains were drawn, and everyone began to wear black armbands as a sign of deep mourning. Our minister, Reverend Mansfield, came to visit us and shared in our grief. Father had been a special friend to him, and the only local person he trusted as a barber for his thick wavy hair. Now he had to oversee father's funeral and burial, and it would be a difficult emotional time for him, as well as the family.

It took about a week for a team of men to travel to St. Anthony and return with father's remains. Snow was still on the ground, especially in wooded areas, but there were also stretches of bare boggy ground, so travel by dog team was challenging. Spring breakup was in progress, and there was lots of ice in the Strait of Belle Isle, so transport by boat was dangerous. Some streams were high with spring runoff and crossing them was also a problem. As with mother's return, a small boat was used to carry the dog team across the biggest stream, and the sled (Komatik) with casket lashed to it, was floated across as carefully as possible.

I remember seeing him in his casket, laid out in the room where my little brother Baxter, and Mother, had previously rested. His head was shaved bare and his body covered with a white shroud. Incisions and sutures were visible on each side of his skull. I remember nothing about the funeral or burial; again, it was such an overwhelming experience that I have blotted the worst details from memory.

CHAPTER 7

After Father's Death

(May 1945)

THE DEATH OF FATHER BROUGHT another dramatic change in our lives as children. We enjoyed stability for two years after he had married Aunt Millie but she could not continue the family unit alone with her fragile health and no income or welfare support. Besides, her father needed her as his housekeeper as Aunt Marjorie was planning to marry.

I was now eleven, and my sister was six. We had been living on credit from our Uncle Isaac Genge, owner of the store which supplied our groceries and other needs, and were indebted to him some $250. In 1945, this was a significant amount, but he forgave the debt and relieved Aunt Millie of that burden. She considered what to do but saw no choice except to allow my sister and me to move next door to live with Grandfather Way. She returned to her father's home to be his housekeeper, and Aunt Marjorie, who had filled this role for many years, married and went to the new house her husband had built. Our old house stood empty for a couple of years, before being sold to a neighbor and moved eastward toward the bottom of the cove. Grandmother agreed on a price of $250 for the house but received only $100 at the time of sale, and nothing after that.

Grandfather Way had a crowd living at his home. His elderly mother, 'Gam', and a teenage nephew, Grant, had been added to his family before us. They had lived next door with Grant's parents who, in 1935, died unexpectedly - within a month of each other - and Gam was too frail to continue living alone. Fortunately, some of the older children had moved away, which allowed some sleeping room for us. My sister and I were accommodated temporarily in a double bed in the upstairs hallway. We accepted and adjusted quickly to our new circumstances. Father's youngest siblings, Aunts Alma and Bertha, and Uncle Henry were teenagers and only slightly older than I, so we blended as brothers and sisters which helped ease the pain of our family breakup.

10. Way family photo from 1936-37. I'm the small boy lower left. Back row shows my uncles and aunts, Pierce, Max, Stewart, Abe, Pearl, Josie, Grandmother and Grandfather. Front row are Bertha, Henry and Alma. Absent is my father, Aubrey.

As summer 1945 approached, Millie and I got settled into our new circumstances and became comfortable in the care of our grandparents, young uncles, and aunts. We returned to school where I completed grade seven and Millie completed grade one. A new fishing season was starting. Grandfather and the older boys did some seal hunting and had caught several harp seals, so we were enjoying some fresh seal meat dinners, and Grandfather was scraping and curing the sealskins so Grandmother could create new skin boots for the coming winter. The cod trap was being prepared for placement in our fishing berth once the ice flows left the Strait of Belle Isle. The boat was painted and readied for launching.

I was eleven and old enough to make a contribution to processing the fish catch. I now owned a pair of high rubber boots so could stand in a boatload of fish and, using a prong, throw the fish onto the dock to be gutted and split. The whole family was soon in the thick of the fishing season and taking advantage of every good day to haul the trap and process the catch. Grandfather was up before dawn checking the weather and tide. Grandmother was getting the fire going in the kitchen stove and preparing breakfast. Grandfather would start shouting to his sons, still in bed upstairs, to get up. When they did not respond, Grandmother would have to go upstairs and rouse them all. And then, the tide and weather being judged suitable, the men were soon in the boat and on their way to the cod trap. About two hours later Grandmother would start looking for the boat and, using grandfather's spyglass, could judge whether it was low in the water with a good catch, or coming back empty. She would then get fresh tea and toast ready for the men, commonly referred to as a 'mug up', to refresh them for processing the catch.

When I returned to school in September 1945, the European war was over, and luxury goods began to flow into Newfoundland. I will always remember receiving our first case of Coca-Cola in school and savoring the taste of this wonderful new drink. The turmoil of the previous four months was behind me, and I was able to resume my studies without too much distraction from bad memories. The crowd at grandfather's house provided lots of emotional support and probably their love and care saved my sanity at this crucial juncture. Returning to school further occupied my day and gave me a purpose to do my best to prepare for my uncertain future.

During the school months, I and my young aunts and youngest uncle did homework together around the kitchen table via the light of a kerosene lamp. Before bed we would play a card game called 'fish' which resulted in much motion, shouting and laughter as we attempted not to be the last person holding a card. Otherwise, I was quiet, studious and reading everything, always inquisitive and observant but not verbally aggressive or athletic. I was still immature and small physically. Everything I saw and heard was analyzed, but I kept my conclusions to myself, and this became my lifelong pattern of dealing with stress.

Even though I was not athletic, I enjoyed participation in soccer. Our school had no gym or indoor facilities for physical activities and no soccer field or playground. However, as children, we always found a clearing for pickup games and sometimes organized teams to play against each other.

My sister and I saw Aunt Millie from time to time as we visited Grandfather Kean's home to play with Annie, Marion, and Wes, - children from his second marriage - who were similar in age to us. Aunt Millie's daughter, little Marjorie, was also part of Grandfather Kean's household as she had remained there during Aunt Millie's time as our step-mother. My sister and little Marjorie enjoyed visiting each other as childhood pals.

Aunt Millie remarried to Harold Whalen about a year and a half after our family split. Other than little Marjorie, she had no other children, but continued to treat us as hers, and loved to have us visit whenever we could. Harold was very kind and welcoming to us as he understood our attachment to Aunt Millie from her time with us as children. Aunt Millie died in 2001, and as I edited this (April 20, 2016), I received the news that Harold died suddenly last evening, after ninety-two years of very kind and productive life. I will always remember his gifts of bottled trout and other Newfoundland goodies when we visited Aunt Millie and him.

Little Marjorie went to England, trained as a nurse in London and worked there a few years before moving to Ireland. In Dublin, she married Philip - a professional watchmaker - and after five years they immigrated to Canada and settled near Halifax, Nova Scotia. She has become like a real sister even though we grew up separated as children and continue to live a great distance from each other.

CHAPTER 8

Living With My Way Grandparents

GRANDMOTHER WAY WAS A REMARKABLE woman who gave birth to thirteen children, eleven of whom lived to adulthood. She suffered in silence through the heavy burdens that she carried within the home. She was a Genge from Anchor Point, a descendant of one of the earliest English settlers in the area, and distantly related to my (maternal) Grandmother Kean, who was also a Genge. She had a very limited education but could write a letter, with assistance from one of her children, and I will always treasure the precious letters she wrote to me after I left home. Every day she was up early to get the fire started in the kitchen stove, and tend to the cow and any other animals she had. After preparing breakfast for the family, she roused the children for school. During the fishing season, she often had to get the young men out of bed and ready to join Grandfather in the boat to haul the cod trap. When the men and children were out of the house, she tended to many other routine chores. She bore the sadness of the

11. Grandmother Way.

death of two infants, one of whom was her last, and before her death, she suffered the loss of her husband, one adult daughter, and two sons.

Grandfather Way was an equally remarkable man but with a vastly different character. He was demanding and hard-driving, something that was a necessity for survival with a large family in an outport environment. He too had little education and could not read or write. He was a tall, thin man with sharp features who wore a long-sleeved woolen sweater, summer or winter, with trousers held up by braces, and rubber boots when outside the house. In the fishing boat, he would wear rubber or oilskin pants and jacket over his regular clothes plus a peaked cap. It was rare to get him dressed up with shirt and tie, slacks and shoes but, for a wedding or funeral, he would usually agree to do so. One of his personal quirks was wearing his woolen socks upside down with the heel on the top of his foot. He was a heavy pipe smoker and used 'plug' tobacco, which came in the form of a small dry brick, from which he peeled off enough shavings with a pocket knife to fill his pipe. He lit the shavings with a match, and he would take several draws as the tobacco glowed. Invariably the flame would require being relit several times over the next hour as the tobacco burned.

12. Grandfather Way in his usual work clothes.

Grandfather was also a consummate weather watcher because trap fishing demanded attention to weather and tides. In winter, when necessary, he would build himself a new boat and the community men always admired his skill in this area. By the time I was eleven, inboard motors had become available for fishing boats, and this required an adjustment in boat design away from the old style sailboats with mast, center boards, and ballast.

A well-traveled Way

One day, Grandfather was in the middle of building a boat to accommodate the new Acadia engine he had ordered, when a surprise visitor came for dinner. Spring was approaching, but the harbor was still frozen, and people routinely walked across the ice as a shortcut from our houses on the south side to the business area on the north. It was a bright clear Sunday morning, and Grandmother had already started cooking dinner for her crew. The menu for the day was special; she was preparing roast caribou meat with all of the trimmings, potatoes, turnip, carrots, pea pudding, turnip greens, 'Figgie pudding' and gravy – all the traditional components of what we called a 'Newfie Scoff.' The roast was well under way and the distinct aroma that caribou meat emitted permeated the entire house. Moose and caribou have special protection on the island – especially the caribou. The regional game warden lived on the other side of the harbor. He was a good friend, and his wife was from the Way family. It was not unusual to have visitors drop in on Sundays and stay for dinner, especially when Grandfather was in the middle of boatbuilding. As the noon hour approached one of the family saw a man walking across the harbor and heading towards the house. Grandfather was lounging on his wooden daybed and smoking his pipe. He was alerted, and a quick look through his spyglass identified the man as the game warden and initiated a household crisis. A diversion was necessary. The young men, still in bed recovering from a late night of courting and partying, were quickly awakened and prepared for a diversionary maneuver. Meanwhile, Grandmother and the ladies were busy ventilating the house and trying to get a fire going in the parlor stove so that dinner could be moved from the kitchen and cooked behind closed doors. As the warden approached the house, all of the men went through the front door to greet and divert him to see the new boat under construction. An hour or more transpired and time went well past the usual dinner hour. It was evident that Stan had no intention of returning to his wife and family, so there was no alternative but to invite him to stay for dinner. When they arrived at the house, the table was set, and dinner was ready. All of the men took their places and Stan joined them at the table. With some apprehension, the ladies put the food on the table as it had been impossible to eliminate the distinct odor completely. Grandfather took the plate of meat and handed it to his guest first with the invitation, "take hold Stan boy, and don't be shy. It's the last of our cow". There were some suppressed chuckles around the table, including from Stan, but nothing further was said and everyone enjoyed the meal.

Grandfather had ordered a five horsepower Acadia engine for the new boat, and the men were anxious for the spring breakup of the harbor ice and the arrival of the coastal steamer. When the *Northern Ranger* arrived to begin her summer season, the engine was on board, and Uncle Max quickly got it installed. I was thrilled to get my first motorized boat ride around the harbor.

About half of my uncles and aunts were at home when Millie and I moved in with them in the spring of 1945, but several were in transition to independent living. Two older sons, Stewart, and Pearce had married and moved into new homes. Two older daughters, Josie and Pearl, had also moved away and, unfortunately, Aunt Pearl had died in 1943. Abe, Max, and Cousin Grant were young single men spending extended times away in the lumber camps, except during the fishing season, and were building homes in preparation for marriage. The youngest three, Alma, Bertha, and Henry were still teenagers and welcomed us like sister and brother. All of my aunts and uncles were a significant part of my childhood years. I was the ring bearer for several of their weddings, and their new homes were welcoming places to visit, especially as their children arrived.

Not all of the family dynamics were harmonious after the marriages. All of the sons brought their new wives into the family home before moving to independent housing. Uncle Stewart's wife was not compatible with Grandmother Way, and this resulted in a lifelong strained relationship. Uncle Pearce married a Catholic lady, and there was concern about her fit in the home, but she proved most helpful to Grandmother, and also to Grandfather because he loved someone who stood up to his quirks and she would take no guff, which endeared her to him. All of the new 'aunties', as

I called them at the time, were kind and welcoming to Millie and me, and their families have continued this relationship.

During my childhood, the family experienced other tragedies besides the deaths of my parents. Aunt Pearl died in 1943. She was one of the most beautiful and gracious ladies in the area at that time. She worked for a time as a clerk in Uncle Isaac Genge's store, but married Nelson Coles in April 1942 and moved to Savage Cove to live with her husband at his parent's home. I participated in the wedding party as ring bearer. The following summer, I spent a week or more living with them and enjoying the friendships of Uncle Nelson's younger brother, Lloyd, and his Cousin Baxter, who lived next door. As pre-teen boys, we spent hours roaming the nearby beach, wharf, and bushes; as we explored, threw stones and picked berries. It was one of the most pleasant holidays of my childhood. Aunt Pearl gave birth to a son, Ross, and shortly after that died of meningitis, leaving the boy in the care of Uncle Nelson and his family.

My Uncle Abe was a strong silent type. He was twenty-three when my father died and worked conscientiously, without complaint, to support Grandfather in the fishery, and with income from working in the lumber woods while he was single. He married a year later and his wife, Rosalind, came to live with Grandfather until they had their new home completed for occupancy. Aunt Rosalind was also a strong lady who, like Aunt Mary, was very helpful to Grandmother and stood up to Grandfather's contrariness, whenever the need arose. I participated in their wedding and enjoyed being part of their life. Uncle Abe built a unique eight-sided house that, as children, we loved to visit because of its nooks and crannies where we played hide-and-seek while it was under construction.

Uncle Max was a year younger than Uncle Abe. He was the extrovert of the brothers and loved to 'stir the pot'. It was his habit to tease his sisters to the point of making them cry and would then walk away while laughing at them. He married Mabel, daughter of Uncle Angus Genge (brother of Grandmother Kean) and had four sons who still live at Flower's Cove. He and Aunt Mabel were very kind to me during my boyhood and throughout their lifetime. Uncle Max was probably most like my father in temperament and personality.

As already noted, Aunt Alma, Aunt Bertha, and Uncle Henry functioned as older sisters and brother to Millie and me after 1945. I spent some time attending school with all of them both before and after father's death. When Aunt Alma was seventeen, she took a clerical job in one of the local stores and lived at home until the following year when she moved to St. Anthony to work as a nursing aid at the Hospital. Aunt Bertha continued attending school with me, finished grade ten and then became a clerk in Uncle Angus Genge's store. She and I shared a desk at school for at least a year. At home, we did homework together and participated in lively games of cards. Uncle Henry dropped out of school at age fifteen as he lost interest or motivation to continue.

In the summer months, as well as pursuing the cod fishery, the family obligations involved procuring a supply of hay for winter, to feed the cow and any other animals Grandmother had. The family owned a patch of hayland about two miles away from the coast, on the other side of a large pond behind our homes. The fields were clearings in the woods, made by the early settlers to serve as a winter homestead in a sheltered area, away from the harsh coastal winds. Remnants of simple living quarters still existed; so we enjoyed roaming through them as children. A trip to the hayland was a daylong adventure over a narrow footpath around the pond. As children, the most exciting activities were participation in stacking the hay after the men had cut it with scythes, and in the noontime picnic around a fire. Part of lunch involved preparing tea by boiling a can of water, containing tea leaves, over the open fire. The tea always had a smoky taste and, with added milk and sugar, was one of the most pleasant tea drinks I ever enjoyed. After a full day, we walked home around the pond over a rocky, uneven, and muddy path. Usually, we made two or more trips to the hay land each year to get the grass dried and stored in a safe way until the snow came and the pond froze. Then we could take a dog team and sleigh to bring it home to the barn.

In 1947, my life took several dramatic shifts. In April, I turned thirteen. In June, I completed grade nine and wrote the CHE (Council of Higher Education) exams set by the Department of Education as the standard for annual advancement through high school. Students in the small outports feared the grade nine exams as they were the first major hurdle to a higher education. Many students would quit school at that point, especially if they failed the exams. Consequently, they sought jobs as store clerks, carpenters, or manual laborers, in preparation for living long-term in an out port. Some became members of the family's fishing and lumbering crew as soon as they were physically mature enough for the heavy work. A few continued at school and repeated the exams the following year with the hope they would succeed. My future was very unclear at this point, even though I was doing well academically. Being advanced by one year at school made me the youngest student writing grade nine exams and, because of this, I was somewhat insecure and fearful of failure. Without parents to guide me, it was unclear what my future was going to be and where I would turn should I fail the exams. My grandparents, with their minimal education, were unable to tutor me and my uncles had all dropped out of school early to become part of Grandfather's fishing crew.

With grade nine exams behind me, there was nothing to do but help Grandfather, and Grandmother, wherever I could and try to stay out of mischief with my chums. However, it didn't take long for trouble to appear. Within a week, I found myself part of a gang of boys who were up to no good. One of my cousins stole a key from a warehouse of Uncle Angus Genge, the senior merchant in town. I was not part of the gang at the start, but a couple of other cousins - everybody was a cousin in Flower's Cove if you went back far enough - were members, as well as Wes Kean, my identical-age step-uncle, who had me added as an afterthought. Thievery was a rarity in such a small outport. The merchants placed keys in their warehouse doors at the start of each business day and left them there until closing time. I am not sure what prompted the theft but, once done, there was an irresistible urge to see what was inside the warehouse. A couple of the boys volunteered to do an exploratory entrance just at dark to see what might be of interest.

BINGO!!!

Much to our delight, several cases of juicy oranges were just begging to be stolen. For the next week or so, our well-organized gang set about extracting oranges each evening and consuming them in the most private spot available – a two-hole outhouse built on the water's edge just behind one of the warehouses. Our organization was well thought out in that two boys, in turn, were assigned to enter the store, two or more provided lookout duty at strategic points, and one handled the key to open and lock the warehouse door for entrance and exit.

All went well for several evenings, and we became bolder with experience. However, Uncle Angus soon noted his dwindling supply of oranges and decided to take action. On the appointed 'fatal' night he went to the warehouse and hid so he could discover how his oranges were disappearing. I was the key holder that night and opened the door for Wes and another buddy and then locked it behind them. I should note that like Wes and I, several of the boys were relatives of Uncle Angus. Nothing seemed amiss, so Wes proceeded to fill the large pockets of his breeches with oranges. Suddenly, Uncle Angus revealed himself and, as a reflex reaction, Wes hauled off and threw an orange hard at him which nearly hit square between his eyes. Several minutes later, I returned to the warehouse door to unlock it and heard Uncle Angus's voice talking to (actually shouting at) my trapped friends. I did not open the door but raised the alarm with my lookouts, and we ran as fast as we could through the town. I ran with one of the others up the road beyond the United Church graveyard to a patch of ground containing some mounds of moss. I kicked over one of the mounds, deposited the key in the ground and put back the moss to bury it. The lights through the windows of nearby houses reflected off the stones in the graveyard as I walked past and I could not help glancing at the markers of my parents, the largest headstones at the time. As I did, I sensed profound shame and remorse over the damage I had brought to their reputation. I knew that if my father were still alive, he would have used his belt on my backside. I headed around the harbor, in the dark, back to Grandfather's house and sneaked into bed as quietly as I could. I don't know how my friends got out of the warehouse, but I presume Uncle Angus let them out after giving them a verbal lashing and forcing them to tell him who was involved.

Next morning, I awoke to animated chatter between Grandmother and other family members who had gathered downstairs. I am not sure how the news came around the harbor so fast, in the absence of telephones, but it traveled like wildfire once Uncle Angus discovered who was involved and spread the word. Grandmother was shocked to hear Cliffy was involved and, by early morning, the whole town was buzzing with the terrible news. I was upset inwardly at being duped into joining the gang and ashamed that my involvement destroyed my image as being timid and 'a good boy'. Eventually, and sheepishly, I had to go downstairs and face the music. My remorse was immense, and I don't recall any of the conversation we had as a family. Afterward, I struggled to function normally, and keep out of further trouble. Frightening rumors abounded that we would all have to stand trial before the magistrate in the fall, and be taken away to jail as juvenile delinquents. The mother of the boy who stole the key went to Uncle Angus in great remorse and pled with him not to have her boy tried or jailed. She was a poor widow and had no resources to pay any fines or penalties. Fortunately, in the days following the crisis, the furor died down. However, Uncle Angus decided not to let the matter die. Even though we were juveniles, he insisted that the traveling Magistrate conduct a court hearing during his next visit. The Magistrate came and conducted the 'trial' in the late fall. However, by then I had left Flower's Cove for high school at St. Anthony so I missed going to trial. The other 'Orange Boys' were all given small fines – which were considered big by some of the parents – and allowed to remain at home. I learned a valuable lesson for the rest of my life. For the next couple of years, I felt like a fugitive on the loose and worried I might be discovered and brought to justice. Some sixty-nine years later, the legacy of my involvement gets rekindled when I visit with family and friends in Flower's Cove.

During the month of July, I was on my best behavior. I tried to be busy as part of Grandfather Way's fishing team by going to haul the cod-trap with my uncles and unloading the fish when needed. By mid-August, the fish were ready for removal from salt bulk for cleaning. I assisted with moving them to the salt water at the beach for washing, and then helped spread them to dry on the flat rocks and, later in the day, gather them in piles to shelter from any rain.

Apart from helping with the fish, I was just a typical thirteen-year-old hanging out with friends, playing games, and developing an interest in girls. The courting ritual in Flower's Cove was probably similar to that practiced in other outports. We observed the patterns of the older boys and learned from them. In summer, the evenings were long and warm. The young people collected at a favorite home and from there would head out on the road for walks. Once on the road the girls walked together with locked arms in groups of two or more and proceeded down the road. The boys would form a group of two or more behind them and gradually close the gap until they were only a step behind. Each fellow would decide the girl he was interested in and, at the appropriate point, would place his hand on her shoulder and tug her backward. If she consented to go with him, she would release her arm locks with the other girls and accept the boy's invitation to walk with him. They usually paused and after a few words headed in the opposite direction for privacy. Another method of courting, in summer, was to organize Sunday afternoon boat trips to one of the islands outside the harbor. These islands had nice grassy areas for a picnic and smooth rocks for sitting and talking. Some had wild berries growing as well as multiple bird nests which were of interest. I participated in the evening walks and also did some Sunday tripping to the islands but was too timid to enter into the dating game beyond being a tempted observer.

During these summer weeks, I was anxiously awaiting the results of my CHE exams for grade nine and also about the pending court case.

During summer 1947, as well, it became fashionable for all of the young people - including the boys - to have their hair curled or 'permed', and I became a victim of the craze when my aunts corralled me into submitting to this procedure. Otherwise, by August, life had returned to normal. The 'orange boys' escapade was receiving less attention - except that Uncle Max did not hesitate to tease me about it, whenever he could.

CHAPTER 9

Another Surprise Transition

(August 1947)

UNKNOWN TO ME, MY TEACHER, Rev. Mansfield, was having discussions with Grandmother concerning my future education. He had been greatly affected by my father's death, having lost one of his best friends in the community, and wanted to see my sister and I well cared for and educated. He felt inadequate to guide me through the final two years of high school at Flower's Cove and was seeking a way to optimize my opportunities for the future.

One day, in mid-August, he came to meet with Grandmother. He advised her that he had been in contact with the Grenfell Mission Orphanage at St. Anthony to see if they would allow me as a resident so that I could complete my high school under their care. The orphanage had agreed to take me, and I could start school in September if she were willing to let me go. She was hesitant to consent but sat down to explain what was happening. I was not ready for another dramatic change

13. Rev. Claude T. Mansfield

so soon in my life but could see the benefit of accepting the educational opportunity. The adventure of traveling on the coastal boat *Northern Ranger* was persuasive and helped me decide to agree to the move. Rev. Mansfield was going to St. John's and could escort me to St. Anthony. Grandmother packed my few belongings into the plywood suitcase my father had made, in preparation for the arrival of the coastal boat. After a tearful parting, Uncle Max drove me in Grandfather's fishing boat to the *Northern Ranger*, anchored outside the harbor rock that guarded the entrance to Flower's Cove. Rev. Mansfield was waiting on the deck and got me signed in as a passenger. I had no berth for sleeping, so I spent the first night on a sofa in the smoking room, and the next I shared a bunk with a small boy whose family consented to this. The boy must not have liked my company because some time later he climbed out and crawled in with one of his parents. I ate in the dining room with the other passengers and was served by uniformed waiters in a rather formal setting. The boat crossed the Strait of Belle Isle to Forteau and then along the Labrador coast to Red Bay and Battle Harbor, before crossing back to the island at Cook's Harbor, with stops at several more ports, before docking at the Grenfell Mission Wharf, St. Anthony. I enjoyed life on the boat, especially visiting the ports I had never seen before and exploring the boat with some of the other teenagers. In spite of the trauma of leaving home, I felt the trip was an adventure and looked forward to my new school and home in a larger town.

St. Anthony is located one hundred kilometers northeast of Flower's Cove, but there was no road connecting the communities until the mid-1960s. It seemed a long way from home after crossing and re-crossing the Strait of Belle Isle and traveling for two days on the boat. I did not see much of Rev. Mansfield, but I was enjoying the ship, the ports along the way, and friendship with other teenage passengers.

CHAPTER 10

Life And School At St. Anthony

St. Anthony was the principle medical center of Northern Newfoundland and Labrador. It acquired this status in 1901 when Dr. Wilfred T. Grenfell built a hospital there and made it the headquarters for his mission work. He discovered St. Anthony in 1892, when he experienced its sheltering embrace on his first voyage to Labrador and realized it was the best harbor in the region. In Labrador, his primary responsibility started out being the medical care of the English fishing fleet, but the needs of the local fishermen and their families cried out to him for far greater attention than those of the fleet. Therefore, he refocused his mission work to meet the needs of the local people. Eventually, this resulted in the creation of an independent mission called *The International Grenfell Association*, supported entirely by philanthropy. Private funds were used to establish amalgamated (non-denominational) schools and

14. Sir Wilfred T. Grenfell, 1865-1940.

homes for children orphaned by tuberculosis and social factors. He recruited hundreds of volunteers to serve as teachers and administrators in these institutions.

Dr. Grenfell was more than an ordinary medical practitioner. As a medical student in London, England, his life was transformed by wandering into a tent meeting and encountering the evangelical ministry of Dwight L. Moody. Moody's ministry to students in London, Oxford and Cambridge, generated a zeal for 'muscular Christianity', i.e., university athletes becoming involved in missionary work. Grenfell was an athlete, and the Christian testimonies of the Studd brothers, star cricket players, convinced him to heed 'the call of Christ' on his life and devote himself to Christian missionary endeavors. After graduation, he joined the *Mission to Deep Sea Fishers* to minister to the medical and spiritual needs of the English fishing fleet, and he crossed with them to Labrador in the summer of 1892. The calling was perfect for him as he loved the sea and was qualified as a mariner. The spiritual aspect of life was an important part of his ministry to the men of the fleet, many of whom were alcoholics. He soon realized too, that the local people rarely saw a Christian minister or priest. So, he routinely said prayers, read scripture and led in hymn singing whenever he visited and stayed with local families, or comforted the sick. I should note that he continued his athletic activity as much as he could, and did not hesitate to swim in the frigid waters of the area, including jumping overboard to retrieve a tennis ball - in mid-Atlantic - on one occasion when he was traveling back from England.

When Grenfell saw the desperate needs and poverty of the local people, he felt directed to serve them as his lifelong work. At the end of his first summer in Labrador, he accompanied the fleet back to England for the winter but in spring 1893, he returned with a team of nurses to establish a permanent hospital at Battle Harbor, Labrador. Grenfell spent the next six winters traveling in England, eastern Canada and the New England States, securing support for his work. In the 1890's, Labrador was impossible as a travel base in the winter months, so he established a winter clinic at St.

Anthony and, with the building of a hospital there, in 1901, this became the headquarters of his work.

Grenfell's winter travels with lantern slides (i.e., slide shows) and stories of Labrador were a sensation. Many churches hosted him for these functions, as did universities, social clubs and prominent financial and political figures. He secured substantial charitable support from generous individuals to deal with the medical and social plight of the settlers in the region. Medical specialists and students at Harvard, Yale, and other schools volunteered to support his activity. These volunteers - referred to as WOP's, i.e., individuals 'With-Out-Pay' - were a great asset to his work in its early days. He moved beyond a simple medical mission into educational, social, business, agricultural and farming ventures. Not all were successful, but the children's home (orphanage), and amalgamated school were outstandingly so. Like myself, hundreds of young orphaned boys and girls were rescued from a bleak future through education and nurture and went on to become significant citizens of the area and beyond.

I was only six years old when Dr. Grenfell died so I did not meet him, but his work extended to Flower's Cove well before my birth. For example, in 1919, he helped the local fishermen form a cooperative business to sell their fish and purchase supplies. In 1920, he built a nursing station with a full-time nurse/midwife to serve the area and refer serious problems to the St. Anthony hospital. Grandfather Kean was a close friend of his. Before the nursing station existed, the Anglican parsonage was used for his clinics. He would stay with the resident priest, Canon J. T. Richards, who was building the historic 'skin boots church' - so called because ladies of the church made sealskin boots and sold them to buy building materials. Grandfather Kean served as lay reader and organist in the church when necessary, and my mother was a faithful worshipper there during her early years. Every generation of the Way family in Flower's Cove benefited from the medical care, and opportunities for work, that flowed from the missionary work of Dr. Grenfell.

A well-traveled Way

In 1947, when I was thirteen, the orphanage and school at St. Anthony became critical components of my future. Both were still staffed, at least in part, by American and English volunteers as teachers and supervisors. The school's students were very successful with the CHE exams, which was why Rev. Mansfield felt I would benefit from attending there for grades ten and eleven. The orphanage provided an exceptional home environment for children whose parents had died or were under hospital treatment for tuberculosis or needed shelter for other social reasons.

By 1947, St. Anthony had become a major center of business and commerce for the area. In addition to the region's referral hospital, there was a large fish plant fed by many local fishermen. The Grenfell Mission's many extra-medical and marine activities were a significant employment source for much of the community. The town was still isolated with only a primitive road around the harbor and over to Goose Cove, some seven kilometers away. There were a few trucks and a jeep owned by the mission for local use but no passenger cars. There were no telephones except for a small private system between buildings in the mission compound, and a simple telegraph at the post office. The mission compound had central plumbing, water, and electricity, but the main town did not have these facilities.

The orphanage was part of the mission compound. The area set apart for mission work included the hospital, wharf and marine dry dock, handicraft building, and several doctor's homes. It also encompassed a garage, steam plant, farm that produced eggs, milk, and beef, a machine shop for making wooden items – windows, doors and even caskets, and gardens for growing vegetables. There was also an annex for housing patients awaiting either transport back home or a bed in the hospital. The school was outside the compound about a kilometer east of the main mission buildings. St. Anthony was a very exciting place for a teenage boy to live and go to school.

Rev. Mansfield helped me with my suitcase and assisted me ashore. On the dock, I was greeted warmly by staff from the orphanage who collected my luggage and took me the short distance to my new home. I had arrived about a week before school started so had time to settle into my new life. It was very different from home. I shared a senior boy's room with eleven others at one end of the second floor. There were six double deck bunks crammed into the bedroom, and I occupied a bottom unit. The older girls had sleeping quarters similar to us but on the third floor. The younger boys and girls slept in larger rooms in single beds and cribs (bunk beds being unsafe for some of them). Each child received clothing appropriate for the season.

15. St. Anthony Orphanage.

I soon acquired some friends, particularly two of the Hodge brothers who were from Flower's Cove, and were living at the orphanage where their mother served as a supervisor. The older brother, Clate, became my classmate in grades ten and eleven and functioned as my protector at school and in the home. He was a funny kid with a rubber face that could make you laugh with just a look and a pose. He and I teamed up in the Christmas play to serve as a puppet. We stood behind a table so that he formed the head, torso, and feet (with shoes on his hands) while my arms and hands became those of the puppet. The interactions of our hands as extremities together with Clate's voice and facial expressions made for a hilarious act. Jim was the other brother. He was the youngest and quieter and more reserved than Clate but was very musical and had a beautiful tenor voice. Mrs. Hodge, as supervisor, was not supposed to have favorites, but Jim was her baby, and she welcomed me as his friend. Frequently, she sneaked Jim and me into her private suite for a cookie and chat. She and her family had been at the orphanage for several years before I arrived. Her daughter and two older sons had already moved out of the home. Clate was also close to moving out and was starting to work at the Mission's farm doing barn chores each day before going to school.

The supervision was provided entirely by mature ladies some of whom, like Mrs. Hodge, were widowed and had children in the home with them. The Senior Matron was Miss Bean, an English spinster, who was respected as a disciplinarian but was also kind and considerate. She tried to teach me piano when she heard me playing by ear, but I only mastered elementary skills and never attained the ability to read sheet music involving both hands. Her assistant was a Miss Zucco, also from England, and I remember her as always wearing hard heel shoes when on duty and the clump-clump-clump of her footsteps alerted us to get in our beds and desist from any mischief. There was a Mrs. Way, a distant relative from Savage Cove, who was also a supervisor and her presence there, together with her two daughters, was a great comfort to me.

The older children were expected to participate in chores which were assigned and rotated monthly. I made my bed daily and changed sheets at the appointed time. In scheduled rotations, I washed dishes, set and cleaned tables, mopped floors, helped in the kitchen, and assisted with the care of the younger children. I did my homework each evening, under supervision, with the other high school students. We enjoyed a variety of entertainment in the form of lantern slides, music, magic shows, board games, etc., during the summer months when medical students and other professionals were present as volunteers.

The senior boys were not without mischief, particularly Clate Hodge and a few others. One of their favorite hijinks was to raid the kitchen in the evening. We were always well fed, but growing boys were always hungry and preoccupied with how to get more. The kitchen and food storage areas were in the basement, and when food was ready for meals, the kitchen staff placed it on a dumbwaiter which, using a rope device, they sent up to the first-floor distribution area. At the end of each meal, any leftover food was returned via this device back down to the kitchen for storage. The kitchen was locked after supper but was accessible via the dumbwaiter and bright boys enjoyed the challenge of riding it down to the kitchen for extra food. Clate Hodge was exceptionally skilled at squeezing himself onto the device for transport. He usually chose an evening when his mother was on duty as the supervisor so that, if caught, he would only have to deal with her. His accomplices, which sometimes included me, were always more concerned about the operation than he was. Most of the time we were able to recover a jug of milk and some bread and peanut butter which, of course, represented a feast. I remember one occasion when we got caught in the act. Clate was half way up, squeezed into the bottom shelf of the dumbwaiter, with the food on the top shelf, when his mother surprised us. We had to complete the operation while she watched. She maintained her usual solemn droll expression in silence, but her eyes told us she was killing herself laughing on the inside. We were scolded and sent to our room without any treat.

I was spared working in the barn or being subjected to any of the farm cleanup jobs although I did my fair share of house cleaning within the orphanage. In the fall of my first year, I was recruited to be houseboy at the home of Dr. Gordon Thomas, the new surgeon at the hospital. He lived next door in a small attractive New-England-style cottage with white clapboard and green trim. It was known as Brown Cottage, in honor of Dr. and Mrs. Lynwood Brown, who had lived there and been supervisors at the orphanage for several years just before my arrival. The Browns provided great parenting at the home, and the older children still remembered them. Some years later, when Dr. Brown was serving as Chairman of the Board of the International Grenfell Association, I was their guest in New England. They were a delightful and loving couple, and I could

16. Me, fall of 1947 at gate of Brown Cottage. Note my hair perm is still present from my aunties in Flower's Cove

see why they were so warmly remembered at the orphanage and throughout St. Anthony.

School life was radically different from Flower's Cove. The High School students were grouped together in a large room on the top floor, and the lower grades had similar groupings. 'Bobby' Gray was our classroom teacher. He had lived at the orphanage and was a survivor of childhood tuberculosis which left him with a fused knee joint. With eyes like a hawk, he instantly detected any mischief in class such as the passage of notes. He was small, slender and fast moving, despite his straight leg, and was a firm disciplinarian. He was a good teacher and was very concerned about preparing us for our year-end exams. He took a real interest in me, and this helped overcome my shyness and insecurity. Another teacher, Mr. Ben Ackerman, taught French. He was a local man, and his father ('Uncle Ben' Ackerman) looked after the furnace and plumbing at the orphanage. Uncle Ben was a kind, grandfatherly figure and a friend to all the children.

17. Original Grenfell School. Scripture on wall states "All thy children shall be taught of the Lord, and great shall be the peace of thy children."

During the summer of 1948, between my two school years at St. Anthony, I was able to go home to Flower's Cove to spend time with my grandparents and visit with my sister. I was able to renew friendship with most of the old gang and enjoyed some good laughs about our escapade with the oranges. I was fourteen and finally beginning to grow and mature physically. Most of my old friends were now focusing on courtship, so we gathered at the home of Joe and Evelyn Rose most evenings and from there would launch our courting ritual. Even though I was a year older, I was not brave enough to enter into this activity with comfort and never did get to date any of the girls.

It was all business to finish grade eleven when I returned to St. Anthony after the summer break. During the fall and winter, I continued to work for the Thomas household as well as do my assigned chores at the Orphanage. I loved visiting the Thomas home each day to check on the supply of wood and coal for the fireplace and tend to any other chores to help the cook. Often I would meet Mrs. Thomas, who was always friendly and chatty and I enjoyed talking with her. Mr. Alex Simms looked after the furnace and heating system, and often he left his small dog in the basement, so I became good friends with the dog. On Sundays, I was expected to make ice cream for the family and their dinner guests. The cook made the mix and placed it in the metal container, and I churned the machine, filled with crushed ice and salt, to make the ice cream before church time. The cook would always give me the dasher (the paddle that churned the ice cream as it froze) to lick, and this was a special treat. The two cooks I served became lifelong friends.

Once, when Dr. Thomas was away from St. Anthony his replacement, Dr. Gordon Erb, indicated he wanted ice cream made for Sunday dinner. I was summoned from the basement and informed of the request, to which I replied rather loudly, "What! Not again!!" The cook blushed, and I instantly recognized that the doctor and his wife were sitting at breakfast around the corner. Needless to say, I proceeded to make ice cream. Years later, when I met Dr. and Mrs. Erb in Toronto, we had a good laugh when I recalled the incident.

I was a faithful attendee at the United Church during my time at St. Anthony. It had been Methodist in Dr. Grenfell's time and was where he had worshiped and preached. Grenfell grew up in a traditional Anglican home, but the evangelical spirit he saw in D. L. Moody, and student athletes in London, awakened his resolve to make Christian evangelism an active component of his life work. That is why he held regular worship services and prayed with people in communities and homes where he visited, even as he dealt with the hungry, sick, and dying.

This 'dabbling' in religion became a somewhat contentious issue later in his work when both church and political leaders complained about his creation of schools and children's homes outside the denominational controls they had established. Further, his exposure of the poverty, malnutrition, and disease in Labrador when traveling to raise funds for his work was openly embarrassing to the government of the day. His exposure of the credit system that enslaved the fishermen was equally embarrassing to the business community. Nevertheless, his impulsive free spirit and conviction his actions were part of the call of Christ made him soldier on for forty years.

The United Church minister during my time was Rev. Peter MacAskill, and he was a very challenging preacher. Dr. Thomas was my Sunday school teacher, and he took charge of a group of teenage boys and taught us well. We all respected him as a role model and viewed him as setting a high standard for Christian living. I had little contact with him when serving at his home as he was always at the hospital or traveling. He was inherently shy and a man of few words but he gave me a New Testament and biography of C.T. Studd, the famous cricket player and missionary, who was a contemporary and influence on Dr. Grenfell. That book was a powerful influence on motivating me also to respond to 'the call of Christ' on my life.

As I finished school in June of 1949, I was unsure of my future. Some of my fellow graduates were planning to become teachers, at least temporarily, and a few were considering the ministry. The Grenfell Mission was funding a couple of the young men to get further technical training so they could return and work as electricians and engineers or equipment maintainers. I considered accepting a teaching job but I was just fifteen, still an immature adolescent, and physically small. Shortly after school ended, I was offered a summer job as cook's helper (Cooke) on the mission's hospital ship *Maraval* which was preparing for its summer trip along the Labrador coast. For the next ten weeks, I had employment, but it was unclear what I would do when September arrived.

My two years at the Grenfell School were very enjoyable. I applied myself faithfully and got a good grounding in most subjects. I felt adequately prepared to leave high school and pursue higher education if the opportunity arose. But such a possibility seemed very remote as my family in Flower's Cove had no money to support me once I left the orphanage. I was only fifteen as I finished grade eleven and had no idea that I would be relocating again, within three months. I was also unaware that the next move would be more stressful than moving from home to St. Anthony and had no appreciation of the shock and stress that the next transition would represent.

CHAPTER 11

Summer On The Labrador Coast

THE *MARAVAL* WAS DIESEL DRIVEN but had two high masts and sails that were available if the engine failed. Each summer the Grenfell Mission sent her along the Labrador coast with a doctor to visit every community to screen for tuberculosis and assess the general health and social needs in advance of the approaching winter. The high masts made her top heavy so that she rolled like a bottle in heavy seas and wind.

Dr. Anthony (Tony) Paddon (1914-1995) was the physician on board. His father had come to Labrador and worked with Dr. Grenfell in the early years of the mission, settled at Northwest River, and stayed a lifetime. Tony was born and grew up there and, after doing wartime (Navy) service, he attended medical school in New York and returned to continue the work of his father and mother. He was greatly loved by the people as he was 'one of them' and fully acclimatized to the native cultures – Inuit, Naskapi, and white. At the end of his career, he was appointed Lieutenant Governor of Newfoundland and Labrador. Indeed, he followed in the footsteps of Grenfell, and his parents, in demonstrating the 'call of Christ' on his life.

The settlers on the coast of Labrador were destitute and lived in crowded houses without central heating, electricity, or plumbing. In the winter months, each small community was in near total isolation and needed to be self-sufficient to survive. Many had no medical services or spiritual ministry and food supply was often short especially in the spring before the coastal boat arrived. Disease, notably tuberculosis, was widespread, and the medical team on the *Maraval* were alert to the probability of active tuberculosis in every resident they saw.

Jim was the cook and gave me my orders for the day. He was easy to work for, and my duties were simple. My time at the orphanage had prepared me for such chores as setting the table for meals, washing dishes, taking tea to the Captain in his cabin, and taking food to any patients housed on the ship. Fortunately, not a lot of meals were served while we were at sea as the *Maraval* rolled with the least provocation and I would get seasick if I stayed below in the galley and smelled food. At such times, I had to go on deck into the cold air to avoid vomiting.

It was an eventful summer. We had just begun our trip northward when a terrible hurricane hit the coast. Many fishing schooners became wrecks, and large quantities of salted cod and gear were washed up on the beach in several communities.

Dr. Paddon and the crew did what they could for the fishermen who awaited transportation back to their homes on the island of Newfoundland. They had lost everything including their livelihood for the next year. A photographer, George Silk, was traveling with us doing a documentary for Life Magazine, and he published pictures of the wreckage later that fall. *(Life, September 19th, 1949, pages 115-124).*

18. Wrecked schooner in Labrador. Boat in distance is Maraval.

I was fortunate to be part of a very friendly crew. Captain Barber was a small, quiet, reserved man who said little. I would bring tea and biscuits to his cabin whenever the cook directed me to do so. The ship's officers, Ted, Jim, and Charlie were wonderful men who cared for the engine and navigated the ship when we were at sea. I was often the brunt of teasing and practical jokes from them, always in good fun. One day, while anchored at Nain, Ted and Jim were on deck enjoying the calm water, and the sunshine, and looking for something to do. I happened to appear and was immediately captured for some mischief. One of them grabbed hold of my arms and the other my feet, picked me up, and suspended me over the side of the ship threatening to dip my rear in the icy water or just let me fall in. I couldn't swim, and the thought of the cold water made my anxiety worse. Fortunately, after a session of panic and screaming they brought me back on board, and I was released. Unfortunately, Charlie the other musketeer was absent as he was my strong protector when the other two got out of hand.

On the last leg of our journey north, we experienced a crisis that nearly resulted in the loss of the ship and our lives. Dr. Paddon wanted to go north, beyond Makkovik, to Saglec Bay to visit an Inuit encampment at that location. He persuaded Captain Barber, against better judgment, to begin the trip even though the forecast was ominous. Half way to our destination the storm struck and we were forced to seek shelter in the lee of a kidney-shaped island (rock) just off the mainland. We anchored in the small cove, but the fierce wind drove sea spray over the highest part of the island and caught the masts of the *Maraval* causing her to drag anchor and, in the darkness of night, we drifted back dangerously close to the rocks. We managed to get the engine going, which kept the boat up to the wind and off the rocks. Two of our crew risked their lives in a dory in the darkness but, aided by a searchlight; they took a lifeline to shore which they secured to keep the boat up to the wind. Unfortunately, the rope did not hold, and we had to depend on the engine for the rest of the night. We were most grateful to the crew and Captain Barber, who saved our lives by their skill during this storm. I spent much of the time watching the action from the shelter of the wheelhouse.

Next morning the wind abated, and we had a beautiful day to complete the trip. We arrived in Saglek Bay and anchored as darkness fell. In the morning, we awoke to find ourselves in a magnificent fjord at the end of the bay. The calm water reflected a single teepee nestled at the foot of the mountain with a column of blue smoke ascending vertically into the sky. Dr. Paddon went ashore and visited a sick lady in the tent. He counseled the husband on her care but could do little else in the situation.

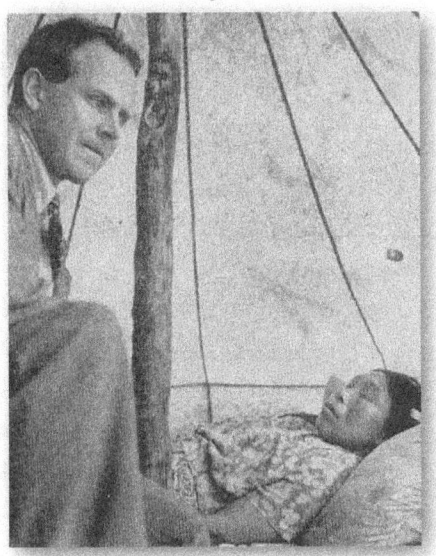

19. Dr. Paddon with patient in tent.

We returned to Hamilton Inlet and docked at Northwest River for a few days to allow Dr. Paddon to visit with his family and do some medical procedures at home base. While we were there, I visited the Grenfell medical facilities and children's home and also made a visit to the Aboriginal village on the opposite side of the river bank. The latter was a sharp contrast to the Grenfell facilities. Some lovely new homes, built by the Government, showed evidence of a vastly different lifestyle. There were bathtubs containing coal for winter fuel, poorly fed dogs tied up in unsanitary areas, and signs of heavy smoking and alcohol use.

We began our return to St. Anthony and stopped at Davis Inlet to pick up a couple of passengers that needed treatment during the winter. They were Inuit and spoke little English. It was very touching as family members came alongside in their boats to say goodbye and sang hymns as they saw their relatives depart. Initially, the patients stayed on deck, but after we were at sea and the weather became rough, it was necessary to have them come below to the galley and eating area. In this enclosed area their sealskin clothing and boots produced a very unpleasant aroma that made my job as cook's helper impossible, so I had to retreat to the rear cabin for fresh air and shelter. It was a great relief to all when, next day, the weather was good, and they were able to remain on deck for the balance of the trip.

For me, the summer had been a great adventure. I gained several new skills and new insights into medical practice in a rural area with limited diagnostic tools and facilities. I was apprehensive about my grade eleven exam results and what would lie ahead for me once they were known. I knew my days at the orphanage would end at graduation, but what was in my future was unclear.

CHAPTER 12

Another Unexpected Move

IT WAS LATE AUGUST WHEN we returned to St. Anthony. I was no longer a resident of the orphanage so continued to live on the *Maraval* for the next week. Our grade eleven results arrived, and I had passed with the best marks of the graduating students. I still had no idea what I was going to do for the future. I was fifteen and too young to enter university. Towards the end of the week, I received a message from Dr. Thomas that he wanted to see me at his home that evening. He informed me that he had talked with Mrs. Charles Curtis (wife of the Superintendent of the Mission), who had agreed to pay for my further education if I wanted to accept her offer. Dr. Thomas also said he had been in touch with a friend, Dr. Arthur Hill, in Sherbrooke, Quebec, who had agreed to oversee what he was proposing. I would travel to Montreal, and then to Sherbrooke, to begin a repeat year of High School in Quebec to get some grounding in Science subjects. It would also take me beyond my sixteenth birthday so I could enroll in a University. A freighter, hired by the mission, would be leaving St. Anthony for Montreal in a few days, and I could go as a passenger.

In 1949, Mrs. Curtis was relatively invisible as a member of the mission staff but, occasionally, I saw her out walking her large black Doberman;

20. Mrs. Charles Curtis

otherwise she stayed in her home on the side of the hill in front of the hospital. Mrs. Grenfell had been her childhood friend in Chicago and, in 1923, invited her to St. Anthony to oversee the recruitment of staff for the hospital, the school, and orphanage. She came and, in 1929, married Dr. Charles Curtis, Harvard graduate and staff surgeon, the most eligible bachelor in town and destined to succeed Dr. Grenfell as superintendent of the Mission. I doubt that she knew me out of all the boys at the orphanage. My later research informed me that her maiden name was Harriett Houghteling, daughter of a wealthy bank owner in Chicago who founded the Brotherhood of St. Andrew, a Christian men's organization in that city. Thus, she had a strong Christian background, something that was never advertised in St. Anthony.

Dr. Curtis had a New England Quaker history and came to St. Anthony in 1915. He heard Dr. Grenfell speak to students in Boston and, like many others at Harvard, was captivated by the stories from Labrador, so he came to see for himself and stayed a lifetime. I met him in 1947 when I moved to the orphanage. He was much more visible in St. Anthony than his wife and presented a stern, gruff, demanding front to hide his pussycat personality. I can say that because I was privileged to travel with him on one voyage and discovered he had a warm, grandfatherly side once he was away from St. Anthony. On the boat, he treated me as his grandson and, at breakfast, teased a young doctor and bride who were also on the trip. 'Did they have a good night?' 'Did the rolling of the boat bother them?' All the while he shook like a bowl of jelly as he laughed, and we did the same while the newlyweds turned crimson with embarrassment. Once we got back to St. Anthony it was business as usual, and the gruff exterior reappeared.

My medical encounter with him occurred on a Sunday morning when I was suffering from a painful boil (carbuncle) on my neck, so I went to the hospital clinic instead of church. After a short wait, the nurse brought me into the examining room. Dr. Curtis appeared after a while, did a quick inspection of the lesion, growled something quietly to the nurse, went behind me and rested a hand near the lesion. Suddenly a sharp, intense pain emanated from my neck. Dr. Curtis dropped something on the table, growled again to the nurse, and left the room. He had lanced (incised) the lesion, and it felt much better once the nurse had cleaned and bandaged it. I still have the scar as proof.

My final encounter with Dr. Curtis was at the end of August 1949 after Dr. Thomas told me that Mrs. Curtis had agreed to fund further education for me. One day I was walking along the road in town when he appeared in his jeep. He stopped, wished me well for my future and said he was glad his wife had agreed to help me. For a few seconds his kind, grandfatherly nature shone through again.

A Telegraph message to my grandparents in Flower's Cove requested permission for my travel to Sherbrooke. Again, I do not recall having any anxiety about this proposal even though it represented a far greater separation from my family than I could imagine. I was at peace within myself and looked forward to this new adventure. When everything was in order, I boarded the boat for Montreal.

The trip up the St. Lawrence River took five days. There were other passengers on board from the mission staff. I remember Mr. and Mrs. Ike Newell as passengers and, although I did not know them, they were very helpful to me in finding my way and meeting my Montreal contact. Mr. Newell had been the manager of the Co-op store at St. Anthony and had also represented the St. Anthony area at the pre-confederation convention in 1948-49. He was on his way to Queen's University in Kingston for further studies and subsequently became a noted poet and Professor of English at Queen's.

It was a very pleasant trip, and I shall always remember my first sight of a train traveling along the North Shore. We passed the beautiful town of Tadoussac and the citadel at Quebec City. Finally, early on Sunday morning, September 11th, 1949, we arrived at the dock in Montreal. I felt the boat bump, and I awoke and decided I should take a look at the city. I went up on deck, and it was still dark, so all I saw was a sea of lights. The sight was somewhat overwhelming to a fifteen-year-old boy from a small fishing village.

    I went back to my bunk for a while, but I could not sleep, and some time later got dressed and joined the other passengers as they left the ship and went for breakfast. With my father's plywood suitcase in hand I walked a short distance from the dock to St. Antoine Street where, with the others, I boarded a tram car to Central Station. It was an overwhelming experience as I entered this massive train terminal and followed the group to the restaurant. We had breakfast together and then Mr. Newell assisted me with the use of a dial telephone (something I had never seen or used) to make contact with Kim Monroe, a medical student at McGill, who had agreed to meet me. After Kim had arrived, Mr. Newell and his wife left for Kingston. Kim helped me purchase a ticket for the trip to Sherbrooke and saw me safely on board. I had never seen a bus before and had no idea how far 145 kilometers was. I was all alone in a strange environment, surrounded by people who were speaking French as well as English, and with no idea what awaited me at the end of the ride. After a very long three-and-one-half hours, and multiple stops along the way, we arrived at the Sherbrooke bus depot. Needless to say, my state of anxiety was very high.

CHAPTER 13

My Year At Sherbrooke High School

(September 1949-June 1950)

IT WAS LATE AFTERNOON WHEN the bus arrived at the terminal. In 1949, Sherbrooke was a city of around sixty thousand people. Its name honors the contributions of Sir John Sherbrooke (1764-1830) to the early history of Canada. He served under the Duke of Wellington in several European wars and was appointed Lieutenant-Governor of Nova Scotia in 1811. He became involved in the war of 1812 and succeeded in capturing a portion of Northern Maine which, for fourteen months, became the Colony of New Ireland. The territory was mostly wilderness at that time and should have become part of Canada to permit a straighter west-east border in the area but, in the treaty that settled the war, it was returned to the United States. The small town that became Sherbrooke was on the western fringe of this wilderness and spanned a valley of the St. Francis River, which ran west to east through the village and served as an important transport route during the war. The river was also a historic trade route for the Aboriginal peoples and early explorers of New France and Canada. In 1949, the city was about sixty percent English speaking and was the commercial center of the region known as The Eastern Townships of Quebec. There was a large English High School in the northern section of the city, and this was where I would be a student.

At the bus terminal, I was met by two young men, Bobby Hill a large rotund teenager who was already balding and Earl Rubley, a tall, gangly young man with a significant speech impediment. Bobby was driving his father's new Oldsmobile and took me to his home on Dufferin Avenue. I was greeted warmly by Dr. and Mrs. Arthur Hill and their other children, Mollie, and David. We chatted for a while, and then had an early meal. They had a French maid, Cecile, who prepared the meal and served us. It was somewhat formal as Mrs. Hill would ring a bell whenever she wanted Cecile to enter the room and bring something or take away dirty dishes. Mrs. Hill's mother, Gran Harvey as we knew her, also lived in their home and ate with us. Dr. Hill was a bit of a practical joker. At the end of the meal, he asked Cecile to bring some cheese. She presented him with a variety, most of which I had never seen before. He proceeded to dish out small samples to everyone – in spite of Mrs. Hill protesting with repeated 'Arthurrrrrrrr's!' When he came to me, he plunked down a moderately large piece of Roquefort! The strong aroma that greeted me was not unlike smelly feet, only worse! His impish grin gave away the ruse, and we all had a good laugh.

21. Dr. Arthur C. Hill.

After the meal, we went to church for their evening service. Dr. Hill was the spiritual leader at Grace Chapel, the local Brethren Assembly, as well as being a medical practitioner/surgeon in the city. His home contained his office on the ground floor and the family quarters were upstairs. The house was one of the oldest in Sherbrooke, a moderately large two-story clapboard structure, painted white with peaked gables above and a long covered veranda at ground level on the front with two entrances - one for the medical office and the other for the living quarters.

The Hills were from London, Ontario, where Dr. Hill's father had established a shoe store. In 1929, the family had visited St. Anthony on the cruise ship *New Northland*. Dr. Hill showed me an autographed picture of Dr. Grenfell – also signed by Lady Grenfell – which hung on the wall of his home. I also learned that he had served as the first General Secretary in Canada of Intervarsity Christian Fellowship and knew Dr. Thomas as a student at McGill in the 1940's. The circle of connection seemed complete as I realized he had met Dr. Grenfell some 20 years before, was a friend of Dr. Thomas, and was familiar with St. Anthony. Years later, he gave me the picture of Dr. Grenfell as a gift and in 2014 I returned it to the Grenfell Historical Society in St. Anthony.

The church service was a different experience for me, but the hymns were familiar and made me feel at home. The preacher was long winded and, after my stressful day, I was glad when the service was over. I met Clem and Lydia Best after the service and was surprised to hear I would be living with them as a boarder. They lived in a southern extension of the city in an area of new housing for veterans who had returned from the war. The Bests had a three-year-old son, Brian. Mrs. Best was an immaculate housekeeper, one of whom you could say that 'cleanliness was next to Godliness.' I feared using the bathroom as it was so clean. Mr. Best was a salesperson for Schroeder valves used in car tires at the time. He traveled extensively to garages in the area. He was a WWII veteran, from New Brunswick, and had fought hand to hand in the streets of Caen during the final assault that recaptured France and led to Germany's surrender.

22. Mr. and Mrs. Clem Best.

They gave me a private bedroom on the ground level, beside the bathroom, which had a small desk and comfortable single bed. Even though it was comfortable, I was lonely and scared, thinking of Grandmother and all my family back home. I missed my orphanage friends too and was worried about how I would cope with the new school. I cried quietly and then fell asleep.

Next morning, Monday was the start of my year at Sherbrooke High School. The school had begun classes a week before I arrived. Dr. Hill came in his car and drove me across town to the school. First, he took me to meet the principal, Mr. Gibson. He was a very kindly man and tried to put me at ease but, naturally, in this strange environment, I was very anxious about what lay ahead. At 10 o'clock it was time to go to my first class. The principal led me to the second floor, and as I entered the classroom, I heard the students and teacher talking in a foreign language, and I recognized it was FRENCH! Mr. Gibson introduced me to the teacher, Mr. Beattie, who led me to a desk on the left and about two rows from the front. The class had already started and was being conducted totally in French. I felt terribly conspicuous and lost! At Grenfell School, I had learned how to conjugate simple French verbs (Je suis, tu est, etc.) but speaking the language had not been required and was not spoken beyond the simplest of words and sentences. In Sherbrooke, the students were comfortable talking in French with the teacher, and I couldn't understand anything. It was a very traumatic experience to have this as my introduction to high school in Quebec. The other classes were more encouraging and conducted in English, but the material was not familiar, especially in science and math. Fortunately, some help and support arrived when Brian Wilcock, a fellow classmate, quickly recognized my anxiety and encouraged me with welcoming friendship. He and his brother, Peter, had gone through the same predicament when they arrived from England a couple of years previously. They invited me to their home after school to share socially and meet their parents. Their family was a great support for me during my year at Sherbrooke High School. Brian and Peter would later follow me to Bishop's University, and then to McGill where we became roommates while we studied in Montreal. When we graduated we went different routes but remained close friends; Brian became a dentist in Vancouver and Peter settled at Edmonton as a pediatrician.

I don't remember how I got back across the city at the end of my first day, but it soon became apparent I was expected to take a city bus, or bicycle, to and from school. There was no independent school bus service at that time. Learning the bus route was stressful but, fortunately, there were other students on board so I could ask or follow the crowd as regards transferring from one bus route to another.

Learning the road by bicycle was another story. I did not know how to ride a bike, having never owned one, so I had a steep learning curve. Sherbrooke is a very hilly city, and I had to ride into a valley, through the downtown area, and then up the other side to get to school. Eventually, I mastered bike riding and could use it as a last resort on days when I was late for the bus, or there were other travel issues. Later on, I discovered my bike came from Harold Munkittrick, who owned a Bicycle Shop. He was a member of Grace Chapel and friend of Dr. Hill. In a few months Harold and Peggy, and their family would become significant players in my life.

The Bests were very kind to me throughout my four months stay with them. Mrs. Best always made me a lunch to take to school and did my laundry as needed. They helped me with sorting out the bus transportation to school each day and, later, serviced my bicycle as needed.

During the first four months at Sherbrooke High, I struggled with French and with the transportation issues associated with getting back and forth across the city. I was lonely for home, found no time for fun things, and was not involved in athletics. On Sundays, I went to Grace Chapel with Mr. and Mrs. Best. I participated in young people's activities at the chapel and attended Sunday school classes each week. Harold Munkittrick was involved in the youth programs, especially in transporting us to various functions in his old army truck. He and Peggy were also involved in running Frontier Lodge, a Christian youth camp owned by Grace Chapel. It was located 40 kilometers south of Sherbrooke at Lake Wallace, an international lake on the border between Quebec and Vermont. Each fall the youth had a retreat at this camp and Harold's army truck was our transportation for the event. Through this, I first became friendly with Harold and his family. I had some wonderful times at various youth activities during the fall of 1949, and this helped me cope with my loneliness for home.

I spent Christmas with the Best's, but when New Year's Day 1950 came, my boarding with them ended. The change came as a surprise and shock as there had been no advance discussion with me about it. I relocated to an old farmhouse on the edge of the city, but it was no longer a farm. It was now the headquarters of Ecole Biblique de Bethel (Bethel Bible School), and I was a paying boarder but not a registered Bible Student. Gone was my comfortable private room. I was given a lower bunk in a shared room with five young men. The students were all devout Christians firmly committed to preparing themselves for ministry in French Canada. The conversation was expected to be in French, in so far as possible, and this was a help in my struggle with speaking the language. I have fond memories of the students as they were sympathetic to my situation and helped me as best they could. The Bible schoolmaster and his wife were strict leaders, and I was expected to observe the house rules just like the students. Getting to school from Bethel was a challenge as there was limited bus service in the winter months and if you missed the bus, your school day got messed up.

I survived the time at Bethel, and in June completed my year at Sherbrooke High School. I managed to matriculate as Mr. Beattie was kind and gave me a mark of 50 in French, just enough to graduate. My other marks were reasonably good, thanks to Mr. Porter, who taught History and Math, Mr. Rockwell, who taught Chemistry and Physics, Mrs. Beattie, who taught English literature, and Miss Hopper, who taught Art. I applied to Bishop's University in Lennoxville, just seven kilometers west of Sherbrooke, and was accepted to begin studies there in September 1950. Mrs. Curtis agreed to continue to fund my education with Dr. Hill as trustee.

When school ended it was necessary to find a job for the summer and Harold Munkittrick came to my rescue. He gave me a job as a clerk in his bicycle shop. More importantly, he offered me a home for the summer, and

I was able to move out of Bethel Bible School and live in his large home on Belvedere Street in Lennoxville. The change was therapeutic as I had a private room again and a family environment prevailed with me being 'adopted' like an older brother to their small son, Dale.

CHAPTER 14

Bishop's University

Living with the Munkittricks
(1950-1954)

THE HOME OF HAROLD AND Peggy Munkittrick was known as a busy hostel for stray youth, so it was not exceptional that they should welcome me. The doors were never locked. Their only child, Dale, was ten years old when I came into their life. Peggy's elderly mother occupied one bedroom, but there were always one or two beds available for 'strays'.

Peggy's life was a whirlwind of activity. She was constantly on the go helping others, as an extension of the Welfare system in Sherbrooke, supplying clothing, food, and shelter to needy families. The phone rang constantly, and she was nearly always searching for people and resources to help the needy. When she got behind the wheel of her car, or Harold's truck, you held on with white knuckles. She would back out of the driveway of their home at the top of the hill on

23. Harold and Peggy Munkittrick, June 1988.

Belvedere Street, and be off in a cloud of dust - pedal to the floor – to bring someone food or clothing or pick up someone who needed a ride to an appointment or shelter. Harold was a quiet 'brick' who absorbed being taken advantage of without ever complaining. He worked late hours at the store and often stopped to help cyclists with a flat tire or a motorcyclist having a machine breakdown. Harold had been a bike racer in his youth and still enjoyed riding his speed bike the 40 kilometers from Lennoxville to his cottage at Lake Wallace whenever the opportunity arose. During the war, he had been a Military Courier transporting information at night on his motorcycle in the blackout darkness. So his bicycle and motorcycle business came as a lifetime natural occupation.

My work at the store consisted of welcoming customers and handling the cash register. I also did some bookkeeping. Harold taught me to drive and then I used his truck to pick up bicycles for repair or make a delivery when the repair was complete. We usually had lunch at Jim's Restaurant a 'greasy spoon' adjacent to the store, and would get home for our evening meal after finishing deliveries and pickups. Sometimes, on a Friday, we would stop at a warehouse and load up groceries and other supplies for Frontier Lodge and then drive to Lake Wallace, deliver the goods, and stay at the cottage for the weekend.

The Munkittrick's son, Dale, adopted me as his older brother and for the next three years I became part of his family, and we became close friends. He was very athletic and during his teen years was heavily involved in track and field at Lennoxville High School. Later, he became a teacher, married and had two children, a son, and daughter who have grown to adulthood and now have families of their own. Later too, in December 1963, Dale and his wife, Annabelle, were attendants at my marriage. Dale died young, but Annabelle continues as a close friend to my wife and me.

In September 1950, I moved into residence at Bishop's University, which was only a fifteen-minute walk from the Munkittrick home. On Sundays, I would ride with them to church at Grace Chapel in Sherbrooke, a drive of about eight kilometers. Sometimes I would stay over with them on a Saturday night and watch the hockey game on TV – something that was novel, exciting, and considered sinful. At the time, the leaders at Grace Chapel viewed television as a worldly device that introduced immoral behavior to the family, so its purchase was discouraged. It was an 'unspiritual' act when Harold acquired the unit for his home. He was nearly relieved of his Eldership when, in the spring of 1951, the device attracted crowds of young people for the Stanley Cup (hockey) playoffs featuring superstars Gordie Howe of Detroit and Rocket Richard of Montreal.

The family always had a dog in the house and, at that time, it was a small boxer. The dog loved to sleep in my bed and would worm his way under the covers to the bottom beside my feet. His presence was very cozy but one night, in the early morning, another guest arrived at the house and when the front door opened the dog let out a loud 'WOOF' and awakened me with a start. On another occasion, the dog was riding home on a motorcycle with Harold and me. We were going at a good pace when Harold suddenly cut speed. The dog thought we were stopping so he jumped off the bike while we were still cruising. He tumbled and tossed for a fair distance behind the bike before regaining his feet, following which he jumped back on the gas tank, between Harold's legs, just as if nothing had happened.

Moving to the campus at Bishop's was an exciting time. A new residence, Norton Hall, had just been completed, and I was among its first occupants. Each room had two beds and two study cubicles with fluorescent lighting. The bathroom and showers were down the hall and served the twenty or more students on the floor. My roommate was Andrew Patton, whom I met at visits with Harold and Peggy. He was from Belfast, Ireland, and had immigrated to Canada and was serving as pastor of two rural Presbyterian churches near Lennoxville. He was several years older than me and very Irish in disposition. He loved to debate or take a contrary position on issues just to heat up the discussion. As roommates, we got along well, but our lifestyles were different. Andrew was very devout and would spend extended times kneeling at his bedside in fervent prayer. This activity was somewhat disconcerting to me as I had never developed such a habit even though I knew I was a Christian. It gave me a bit of a guilt complex and meant I had to check his status quietly every time I came and went or wanted to talk or make any noise in the room.

Andrew's Irish heritage meant he had a good sense of humor, as well as being 'religious', and he made many friendships through practical jokes. One day one of his friends decided to play a trick on him. Andrew was enjoying a hot shower, so the friend got a bucket of cold water and threw it over him. A chase ensued up and down the three-level-glass stairwells at the ends of each floor and facing the front quadrangle of the campus. The chase ended when Dr. Gray, the dour Professor of English, and Warden of the residence, opened his apartment door at the bottom of one stairwell and confronted the naked Andrew. Even Dr. Gray found it humorous.

Andrew had a lovely tenor voice and was frequently asked to sing at the worship services of Grace Chapel. His favorite song included the following verse -

> "I am a stranger here, within a foreign land,
> My home is far away, upon a golden strand,
> Ambassador to be, O'er lands beyond the sea
> I'm here on business for my King."
> [*Words by Elijah T. Cassel, (1902)*]

The three years at Bishop's seemed to go very fast and were very enjoyable. Because of my weak grounding in most subjects, especially the sciences, I struggled to keep up and maintain good grades. I was average in physics (Professor Holmes) and biology (Professor Langford) and a little better in chemistry (Professors Kuehner and McCubbin). I was not strong in English (Professors Gray and Motyer) but managed to cope. I stayed away from French. In mathematics (Professor Richardson) I also struggled as, like Professor Holmes, he tended to roll two or three steps into one when he outlined the solution to a problem, expecting everyone to have the background of three years in the subject in a Quebec high school.

Ancient history was a breeze as Professor Preston was blind and did not know if you were in attendance or not. I was too small to be competitive and participated timidly in floor hockey but was otherwise just a spectator at sports events.

In summer 1951, I worked for Harold in his store and returned to living at his home. I would go to the cottage on weekends and share in waterskiing and boating with Dale and other family members. Peggy's brother and family often came from Montreal for weekends, especially holidays, and there were always additional young people or whole families around as guests. Several other members of Grace Chapel had summer cottages, and their children made for a busy social life. I attended many of the Christian worship and expository meetings held at Frontier Lodge during this time.

In summer 1952, the Grenfell Mission decided to have me return to work for them, helping complete the Sanatorium under construction as an addition to the hospital. I traveled from Sherbrooke to Halifax by train and, at the dock, the mission's boat, *Nellie A. Cluett*, accepted me on board for the three-day trip to St. Anthony. I worked as a general laborer for Mr. Ted McNeil, Superintendent, and was mainly involved in laying the steel rods for the two levels of flooring. I remember a particularly frustrating problem we encountered. The rods were all one inch too long, so they had to be shortened by that amount, and this was a difficult job, causing Mr. McNeil lots of frustration and anger. Eventually, we got through the extra work involved and poured the cement floorings after some delay.

At the end of the summer, I was given time off to visit my sister and the Way family in Flower's Cove. For the return to Nova Scotia, I was picked up by the fishing schooner, *Marjorie Inkpen,* at Flower's Cove. The five-day trip was one of the worst I ever experienced, as I got seasick early in the voyage and could not recover. It was made worse by the diesel exhaust fumes entering my bunk area via a porthole, and the terrible food offered. We had bread, tea, and roasted dried capelin for practically every meal. I was never so glad to set foot on land. From Sydney, I took the Acadian Bus Lines and traveled for the next forty-eight hours to Montreal and then to Sherbrooke.

I was exhausted when I arrived back at the Munkittrick's home and needed a good sleep to recover.

In the middle of my final year at Bishop's, I applied to McGill University in Montreal for medical school entrance. I believe the application went in before the Christmas break. In January 1953, just as I was returning for my final semester, I received the news that Mrs. Curtis had died. A short time later I was informed that no funds would be available to pay for finishing my year. Fortunately, a way was found for alternate funding which allowed me to complete the year and graduate with my B.A. degree. The University Registrar was a close friend of Dr. Hill and the Munkittricks. He was a Rotarian and persuaded the Rotary Club of Sherbrooke to loan me $400.00 to cover my expenses through to Graduation.

24. Visiting with my sister, Summer 1952.

In February, I received notice of my acceptance in Medicine at McGill for the class beginning in September. As wonderful as the news was, I was in turmoil as I had no funds to pay my way. Through the help of Professors Keuhner and McCubbin, I found a job as a chemist with Canada Paper Company at Windsor Mills – about 20 Kilometers east of Sherbrooke.

McGill allowed me to defer entrance into Medicine for a year, giving me fifteen months to earn money to pay for my first year there.

Graduation at Bishop's in 1953 was an exciting day. The convocation speaker was John Diefenbaker, Prime Minister of Canada. Andrew and I graduated (BA) together. We had become adoptees of Harold and Peggy, who supported us at such events as 'family', as did several others from Grace Chapel. They held a reception for us, and we received gifts to mark the event. I received a doctor's bag as a special gift.

25. Graduation photo, Bishop's University, 1953.

Early in my three years at Bishop's, I had come under strong Christian conviction. I knew I had made a personal commitment to Christ through reading the life of C.T. Studd, the book given to me by Dr. Thomas in St. Anthony, but it was during my seventeenth year that I rededicated myself to following 'the call of Christ' in my life. I enjoyed the Bible study times conducted by Intervarsity Christian Fellowship on campus, led by Dr. and Mrs. Donald Masters. Dr. Masters was the distinguished Professor of History at Bishop's. Also, I remained under the influence of Grace Chapel and Dr. Hill, who was the trustee for my funding at Bishop's.

I remained unsettled by the death of Mrs. Curtis and loss of financial support but felt that, if God wanted me to become a doctor, He would work out the details as, thus far, He had provided the people and resources I needed to guide and support me.

CHAPTER 15

Windsor Mills

**Work at Canada Paper Mill
June 1953-August 1954**

―∽―

AT GRADUATION, I MOVED OUT of the residence at Bishop's and my home was again the Munkittricks, even as I worked twenty kilometers away at Windsor Mills.

Windsor Mills was a typical one industry town. There was a large paper mill, surrounded by piles of logs, belching out steam and hydrogen sulfide. The mill dominated the roadside as one entered the town, and depending on the wind; you could smell it a mile or so before you saw it. The adjacent St. Francis River had been a water route for Native tribes and early French explorers. It flowed through Lennoxville, past the campus at Bishop's, then through downtown Sherbrooke, before passing through Windsor Mills and winding in a northwest direction to empty into the St. Lawrence River, just east of Sorel. A whistle blew at the start and end of work shifts at the mill and was audible throughout the town.

For the workweek, I found a boarding home with Charles and Marie Gagnon, which was within walking distance to the mill. They spoke limited English, so I had to communicate using the small amount of French I had learned during the previous four years. The Gagnon's lived in an upstairs flat and had a room that I sometimes shared with a second border. Usually, the other boarders were short term guests visiting the mill from other countries such as India, so they were more at a disadvantage than I as regard language. Charles said little, but Marie was very talkative and loved a good joke. They were childless, and this was an obvious sadness to them. They had a large extended family within the town and relatives frequently dropped in for tea or beer. The conversation was lively and noisy during those times. They were devout Catholics, and I heard them saying the Rosary on many occasions. Marie made me a lunch to take to work each day.

I took a bus to Sherbrooke on Friday night after work, and Harold Munkittrick would pick me up, or I would get let off close to his store and then go home with him. Peggy would wash my clothes and try to get rid of the hydrogen sulfide smell they acquired from my working in the mill. On Sunday evening, I would return by bus to my boarding house to be ready for work next day.

I worked as a chemist in the control lab. The lab monitored the recovery and dumping of chemicals, chiefly sulfates, and phosphates, used or generated in the paper making process. Each day a report would be produced showing the results of our tests and, based on the water flow into the sewer system, we calculated the chemicals recovered and lost. Needless to say, the lost chemicals flowed directly into the river which was heavily polluted downstream from that point. Environmental protection was not a concern in 1953. We had a set of guidelines as to what the chemical levels should be in sampling areas, and if our results were too far outside the 'control' limits, then one of the senior chemists would 'adjust' the report. The others working in the lab were long-time employees and how much chemistry they knew appeared questionable. Most of the testing was complete by early afternoon of each day, and several of the senior men spent the last hours of 'work' nodding at their desk or socializing and smoking. The lab supervisor, Michael Turner, was very fair and did his best to keep things running smoothly. He was very kind and accommodating to me even though he knew I was a short-term employee.

I enjoyed spending weekends with the Munkittricks at their home or cottage during the fifteen months I worked in the mill. Holiday times, notably Thanksgiving and Christmas were special. Peggy was generous with gifts and meals and always had a crowd during holidays.

In late August 1954, I completed my time at Windsor Mills and prepared to move to Montreal for medical school. I had sufficient funds to pay back the loan from the Rotary Club and also pay for my first year at McGill. In retrospect, I cannot help reflecting, once more, on how good God has been in supplying for my every need.

CHAPTER 16

McGill Medical School
And
SUMMERS ON THE SAGUENAY CRUISE
(September 1954 - June 1958)

I WAS EXCITED, YET APPREHENSIVE, about finally moving to Montreal and Medical School. Other than a short visit in late 1952, to attend an entrance interview at McGill, I had not been in Montreal since September 1949 when I landed by boat from St. Anthony. Five years had passed since the Sunday morning I had breakfast at Central Station, was met by a McGill medical student who bought my ticket and guided me to the bus departing for Sherbrooke. I was now twenty years old.

My home for the next four years would be Student House at 3445 Peel St., close to the McGill Campus. This residence was operated by Intervarsity Christian Fellowship and served as headquarters for their ministry on campus. About twelve young men lived on the upper floors. The main floor consisted of a dining area and a moderately large front room with fireplace, sofa, and chairs. In the basement was the kitchen and living quarters for the cook, plus a small bedroom which was occupied by one female student. Mrs. Jordan, a lovely senior lady from Jamaica, served as the cook. Her son, Bob, also lived in the house and was the manager when I arrived. He gave me the job of treasurer and bookkeeper, and this allowed me free room and board. Bob was already an engineer but was starting medicine in the same class as me. At meal times, several outside students would join us to provide a lively international conversation around the table. We had an Egyptian student who was understandably vocal over the hot topic at the time, namely the Suez crisis, i.e. the Egyptian takeover of the canal operations from Great Britain and France. We were a mix of medical, engineering, arts, and theological students; all young men except for Ruth, the student who occupied the basement bedroom. Being also from Jamaica, she served as a companion to the cook and tended to eat with her. The young men, including myself, represented diverse backgrounds and we debated and shared our perspectives on the topic of the day.

On Sunday evenings, there was often a hymn sing and a guest speaker who gave a short Christian expository talk. In my time, we had visits from Wilbur Sutherland, Tony Tyndale, Grace Layman and others who were in leadership with the Intervarsity Christian Fellowship organization. Local faculty members such as Dr. C.P. Martin, our Professor of Anatomy, and his son, Dr. John Martin, also came as invited speakers on occasion. John was a rheumatologist at the Montreal General Hospital, and some years later he went to Newfoundland as a faculty member at Memorial University while I worked there.

I shared a room with brothers, Peter and Brian Wilcox, whom I knew from Sherbrooke High School and Bishop's, so this made life more enjoyable. Peter was a year behind me in medical school, and Brian was in the dentistry program. Again, at holiday times, I would take a bus to Sherbrooke and visit with the Munkittricks for some family life and social times with the young adults at Grace Chapel or Lake Wallace.

In the summer months, I enjoyed a further adventure. A friend encouraged me to apply to Canada Steamship Lines to work on their Saguenay Cruise ships. A Mr. Bernier interviewed me, and I was accepted to work as a Bellhop on the *SS Richelieu*.

Each cruise was for seven days down the St. Lawrence River with stops at Sorel, Quebec City, Murray Bay then east as far as Point aux Pere, Tadoussac on the north shore and into the Saguenay River to Chicoutimi. Half way along the Saguenay River we came to Cape Trinity, and when we passed after dark, we stopped to beam the ship's spotlight on a statue of the Virgin Mary located on this high point of land on the western shore, and the band would play Ava Maria. At Chicoutimi, I served as a guide for a bus tour of the Shipshaw power plant and the Aluminum Company's hydropower dam. On the return trip, I enjoyed stopping at Murray Bay (now called La Malbaie) to benefit from the facilities of the Manoir Richelieu. The Manoir was a large Canadian Pacific Railway resort, filled with historical Canadian art which I loved to explore, and there was also a beautiful swimming pool that I was allowed to use. At Quebec City, I had free hours to enjoy the ramparts, the Chateau Frontenac, the surrounding museums, artwork, and restaurants. Occasionally I visited a family from Frontier Lodge and enjoyed an afternoon socializing with the young adults.

In September 1955, I came back from my first twelve week stint on the Saguenay Cruise and returned to Student House to start the second year of medicine. Anatomy, Histology, and Biochemistry were behind us and a whole new set of subjects – Pharmacology, Pathology, and Jurisprudence – were introduced during the first term. After the Christmas break, we began clinical bedside sessions with training in history taking and physical examination. Overall, the load was lighter, and I coped without difficulty. I enjoyed holiday breaks with the Munkittricks, especially at Christmas and Easter.

26. Me, as Deck Steward.

For my second and third summers between the medical school years, I returned to working on the cruise ship. I was given a new job as a Deck Steward and shared responsibilities with two other medical students, Herman (McGill), who went on to become a psychiatrist in Toronto, and Andre (U de Montreal) who became a rheumatologist in Sherbrooke. The work was very pleasant. We tended on the passengers relaxing on the deck chairs. We had a supply of blankets to wrap their legs when the weather was cold, and also, we brought them drinks from the bar during warm days. At the end of each day, we would stack and cover the chair cushions to prevent them from getting wet. At the end of each week, we moved all the chairs to allow washing of the deck and then replaced them in position afterward. Every week we cared for a different group of young adults who occupied the deck chairs. It was always pleasant to get to know them and share socially on shore outings, during bus rides and the weekly bonfire that we supervised while in port. During bus tours, I continued as a guide and provided a running commentary on points of interest as we went along. Being able to spend summers working on the Saguenay Cruise served as a source of fulfillment socially during my medical school years.

At the end of each summer, I returned to Student House to resume the responsibilities of treasurer and bookkeeper and enjoyed free room and board as a result. There was abundant social life on campus and at churches, if I needed it, and I sustained my Spiritual life by walking the short distance to People's Church on Sundays. My previous experience on the *Maraval* in 1949, proved valuable preparation for the summers I spent working on the cruise ships.

Everything considered, my four years as a medical student were most enjoyable. Each summer I made enough money from tips to pay for my books and other needs during the subsequent school year. I never lacked for clothing as Peggy Munkittrick was always giving me items as gifts. One year she obtained a supply of clothes donated by Ocean Pacific, a large supplier of sportswear, and Dale and me, and several others were decked out in colorful striped T-shirts, swim trunks, and other items that made us look like a work gang from prison.

CHAPTER 17

The Medical School Experience

(1954 - 1958)

THERE WAS ONLY ONE PRESSURE point at McGill, and that was the medical school itself. I was part of a class of 100 students, about 50 of whom were from the USA and the balance from points across Canada. I was the only Newfoundlander, and there were only two female students. For anyone who has the privilege of becoming a medical student the first day of classes is always memorable, but this was especially so at McGill when the old classic curriculum existed.

In 1954, the first year at McGill was entirely classroom learning. Bedside teaching and learning to interview and examine patients began during the second year. Our first class began with a welcome by the Dean of Medicine. He introduced the Professor of Anatomy, Dr. C.P. Martin, who promptly began to describe, with detailed chalk drawings, the anatomy of the arm beginning at the neck nerves (brachial plexus), muscles and blood vessels and extending down to the elbow. I should note that, in the previous months, having been forewarned of what lay ahead, I tried to prepare myself for anatomy class. Dr. Hill gave me a copy of *Gray's Anatomy*, published in the 1920's, from which I tried to memorize the names of muscles and nerves. But it proved of no value because the old book had

Latin names for everything and now English nomenclature was in use. Dr. Martin was a master teacher and artist and liberally provided acrostics and other tools to help us memorize anatomical parts. After his hour was complete, he was replaced by Dr. C.P. Leblond, Professor of Histology, who gave an introduction to Histologic procedures and basic anatomy of human cells. Then followed the third lecture by a professor who introduced us to the concepts of cell physiology. It was now noon, and I was hopelessly drowning in information and knew I would never catch up. But, there was more to absorb!

Dr. Martin Banfill, in charge of the Dissection Laboratory, arrived to tell us our group assignments for work in anatomy dissection. He solemnly addressed us on the ethics of respect, confidentiality, and reverence for the human bodies we were about to handle. He then led a quiet apprehensive class into the dissecting area where at least 20 cadavers lay on tables covered by white sheets. The room smelled strongly of formaldehyde and death. It was a solemn occasion for all of us as we approached the moment when we would pull back the sheet and see the body for the first time. A prosector came around to each group and gave courage by showing a dissection already done. Each student received a manual showing how to dissect each area and once we started and got the feel of tissues we were able to continue without difficulty. A lab assistant wandered around between the groups and helped us progress on schedule. At the end of each session we were expected to tidy up and wrap the body in fresh preservative before leaving. It was hard to remove the smell of formaldehyde and death from one's hands at the end of the session, despite repeated washings before and after leaving the dissection area.

After each part of the body had been presented in anatomic detail – the arm took about a month in the first instance – we received notice that a 'spot' exam was on our schedule. This test consisted of a series of dissections with a pin stuck in some part of the specimen, and a nearby card had a question to be answered. You had ten seconds to read and answer; then a bell would ring, and you were required to move to the next specimen to let the student behind you have his ten seconds. Then the bell would ring again, and everyone had to slide along through the questions. I was never good at this type of exam and, need I say, my nervous and fatigued state impaired my performance but I did get a passing mark.

In addition to the overwhelming experience and information associated with anatomy, we had to remember the details of histology and biochemical processes in the body. I used every waking moment trying to cope, catch up and keep up. I found it necessary to set aside any non-medical activity, and when Thanksgiving came, I chose to stay at Student House rather than travel to Sherbrooke for a break. But, when Christmas arrived, I was more than ready for a week with the Munkittricks. The second half of the first year went more smoothly, and I passed all of my exams and was allowed to proceed. Five of my classmates failed.

The medical program became more comfortable as I moved through the four years. The major subjects taught during the last two years were pathology, bacteriology, and pharmacology. With each new year, my time increased on the wards, in clinics, and in emergency and routine care. I think my strengths were in clinical skills, except for psychiatry which I found lacking in scientific basis in some areas. The exams held at the end of the fourth year were clinically focused, so I did fairly well and graduated without difficulty.

Graduation from McGill was a very special occasion for my family and me. Aunt Selina came from Corner Brook to be with me. Harold and Peggy Munkittrick also honored me with their attendance. The *Montreal Gazette* published a feature article on me, including photos taken by Gordon Pritchard, their

27. With Peggy Munkittrick and Aunt Selina (Kean) Headge, Montreal, Spring 1958.

chief photographer. Gordon was married to Blanche Whalen, who also grew up in Flower's Cove, and their home in La Salle was a frequent source of support during my years in Montreal. I was fortunate to have several other members of the Whalen family in Montreal that I could visit if I needed a break or a social outing. I took Aunt Selina to visit some of them, and they were delighted. Also, Con and Mattie McGregor and their young family were living in Montreal at that time and seemed to love to have me visit them. Con's mother was a Slade from St. Anthony and he attended Grenfell School a few years before me. Mattie was a Hodge from Savage Cove and a relative of the Hodge family at the orphanage. Their home provided great comfort breaks in times of loneliness and stress.

During the fourth year, I was asked to submit preferences for internship and was fortunate to be selected by my first choice - the Montreal General Hospital (MGH). So, on July 1st, 1958, I moved from Student House to the MGH house staff residence on Pine Avenue on the side of Mount Royal, a breathtaking location overlooking the city and St. Lawrence River. The facilities were only four years old, very lovely but not air conditioned. The food was excellent and always available in the kitchenette as house staff worked around the clock. We received uniforms (whites) and had free laundry services. The typical schedule for the year as Rotating Interne was to spend two months on various services such as Medicine, Surgery, Obstetrics, Pediatrics, Psychiatry, and Emergency Clinic. The MGH also offered an option of two months in Bermuda or North Carolina.

28. As MGH Interne and Resident, 1958-60.

In my case, I spent two months at Memorial Hospital, Charlotte, North Carolina. This placement was a very educational experience. My assignment was in September, and the humidity and heat were still intense. I can remember the heat radiating from the parking lot as we walked to our residence at the end of the day. The living quarters were not air conditioned, so we used fans and wide open windows as ways of reducing the heat for sleeping. Fortunately, it did cool down at night, so this helped. Duty call was every second night plus the regular full day and every second weekend. It was still the era of segregation in the USA so the hospital served only white people except in extreme emergencies when a colored person would receive care until they could move to the Good Samaritan Hospital – a much inferior facility. I shall always remember an embarrassing incident which occurred while getting on a bus with two colleagues. They were ahead of me and took the second-row seats. I, innocently, took a place available in front of them but beside a black lady. She became very uncomfortable and mumbled something and then moved to a seat further back. I suddenly realized I had embarrassed her by sitting beside her, something that was not acceptable in the southern culture at that time. My Canadian innocence had caused a problem.

I remained at the MGH for another year as a junior resident in Internal Medicine. The rotations now shifted to subspecialty areas such as neurology, cardiology, endocrinology, and gastroenterology. Duty call was more tolerable being every third night when manpower permitted. Working hours began to create less fatigue and social life outside the hospital was more enjoyable. I began to attend young adult functions at People's Church and appreciated the time spent with nursing staff and fellow residents. During the year, I made the decision to move my training in the direction of Pediatrics. Also, I decided that a year outside of Montreal would broaden my educational experience. I applied for a pediatric residency at the Vancouver Children's Hospital and was accepted.

In the spring of 1960, I was completing my time at the MGH and preparing for Vancouver when another exciting development came into my life. I had started to attend Snowdon Baptist Church and became integrated into the active social life of their young people's group. I dated a couple of the young ladies but one, secretly, was of particular interest. Betty Milne had been a girlfriend to a couple of my buddies, and when I discovered she had terminated her latest relationship and was free, I decided to screw up my courage and ask her for a date. I was fearful of being refused because I was eight years older than her and she was just finishing high school and applying for training in nursing. At Easter time, a performance of Handel's Messiah was scheduled for Montreal's historic Notre Dame Cathedral, so I invited her to accompany me to the performance.... and she accepted! We enjoyed each other's company, and we saw each other again at church and Sunday dinners – her mother took to inviting me to these – but I cannot recall that our romance progressed much in the weeks leading up to my departure for Vancouver. We did agree to write each other and keep in touch that way.

29. Betty as student nurse.

CHAPTER 18

A Year In Vancouver

(JULY 1960 - JUNE 1961)

I WAS ABLE TO BUY a car at the end of my residency at the Montreal General. My pay, only $25.00 per month when I started there, had increased to $250.00 in my second year; thanks to a province-wide strike by the house-staff. I was able to purchase a 1952 Chevrolet, which served me well for the next few years including my travel west to Vancouver and back to Montreal. I had graduated from McGill debt free because of the tips from my summer job with Canada Steamship Lines. Also, the free room and board at Student House for the four years of Medical School helped keep my expenses low. I cannot help but reflect on how wonderful God was in supplying my needs during those years, and has continued to meet my needs through all of life!

I arrived safely in Vancouver and checked into the house staff quarters where I received a spacious corner room. Again, laundry and meals were free, and my pay was similar to what I received in Montreal. It was lonely, but I settled into the new surroundings and fitted in well with the pediatric staff and trainees. It seemed more clinical and less academic than the Montreal environment, but I was happy to be out from under the scrutiny of some former supervisors, notably the Physician-in-Chief at the Montreal General. The pressure of work was no less, but we were given greater freedom in decision making, and working with children was far more pleasant.

I sought out a church to attend and received a warm welcome at Ruth Morton Baptist Church where I found great fellowship and companionship with their young people for the year. For a continuing taste of family life, Bert and Marion McGee quickly opened their home for regular visits. Bert grew up in Sherbrooke as part of the youth at Grace Chapel, had attended McGill, and his sister was one of Dr. Arthur Hill's secretaries. He was now a high school teacher in Burnaby. Marion was a graduate nurse but was then busy full-time with family. They had four beautiful children, two boys and two girls, all in their preteens, and their home environment was an oasis to me as I had no other friends or family nearby.

30. Bert and Marion McGee and three of their children. A fourth arrived later.

Work at the hospital became routine once I adjusted to the new surroundings and knew the staff physicians and nurses. Working with children was a much more positive experience than dealing with adults. As a caregiver, you had to be much more upbeat and cheerful even though you sometimes worried about the outcome of their medical problems. I enjoyed dealing with the newborns and developed skills for inserting small scalp vein needles and doing other technically challenging procedures. The hospital had one large room for treatment of respiratory illnesses such as croup and asthma. The children were in beds, cots, or oxygen tents with the whole room drenched with a cool mist fed in by pipes in the ceiling. Dr. Harry Baker, one of the senior staff physicians, had designed the room, and it was unique to this children's hospital. I am not sure that it was any more effective in treating the children than individual tents or mask therapy, but the water-laden atmosphere kept their bedding soggy and requiring frequent changes. In another area, there was a room full of children in iron lungs as there had been an outbreak of polio in the northern part of the province and children were flown in for emergency care and respiratory support. I had to take my turn with other trainees in the constant monitoring required by these patients.

I wrote a letter to Betty soon after my arrival and thus began a steady stream of correspondence across the country. We wrote each other at least weekly, and there were additional phone calls from time to time. As a result of this communication, our romance deepened and our love for each other grew. By the time the year was over our relationship was serious and getting back to Montreal had some urgency and excitement. I drove back as fast as I could, dipping down into the USA in Manitoba to pass through North Dakota, Wisconsin, and Minnesota. Then it was on to Illinois, through the Southside of Chicago – a scary drive at the time - on into Michigan, Ontario, and back to Montreal.

CHAPTER 19

The Montreal Children's Hospital

(July 1961-1964)

It was exciting to be back in Montreal because of my developing romance with Betty and also because I was returning to the Montreal Children's Hospital where I had loved working as a student. I had made friendships with senior hospital staff who were most welcoming on my return. Dr. Allan Ross was Chief of Pediatrics, and he was a soft-spoken and charming physician who was loved by all of his residents. Many of his staff were national leaders in their specialty areas.

In my first year back, I functioned as a senior resident on the wards and gained additional experience in dealing with many common as well as complex conditions. I attended daily patient rounds and weekly grand rounds and guided the most junior trainees in admitting and managing patients. I used my technical skills as needed to support others in doing procedures on children. I did journal research on whatever disorders we were dealing with and shared the information at rounds with the trainees and staff. My work schedule was lighter at having to be on-call only every third night and third weekend. My journal reading was in preparation for the Royal College Fellowship exams which all trainees were expected to take, and pass, to gain recognition as a specialist.

As my second year began, Dr. Ross invited me to share the duties of Chief Resident in Pediatrics with my colleague, Dr. Colin Forbes. We split the year by spending six months on inpatient services and six months in the outpatient area. Our extra duties involved schedule planning for the house staff and reporting to Dr. Ross daily on any issues such as persons absent due to sickness. We also had to make sure the trainees attended daily rounds and made proper chart notes on patients regarding management, investigations, and medication changes. Finding beds for new admissions was always a problem, so we had to pressure staff to approve patient discharge as soon as possible. It was our duty to plan weekly grand rounds by preparing a topic, sometimes illustrated by a patient's case presentation. During grand rounds, the senior staff gathered in the main auditorium to hear the presentation and shared in questioning the presenter and providing experience input. Sometimes a literature review had to be presented on the subject discussed. Such performances helped sharpen our critical appraisal skills and academic analysis of data, important abilities necessary for our Royal College Fellowship exams and our future as independent consultants.

As the second year ended, I was intensely preparing for my first attempt at writing the Fellowship exams. The written part took place in November, half way through my third year, and I passed; however, I failed the case presentation (oral) part and was only granted Certification in Pediatrics. For the third year at Montreal Children's, I had accepted to be a Fellow in Pediatric Cardiology with Dr. Arnold Johnson and his staff. Remaining for the third year was a wise choice as it enabled me to be in an academic environment at the time I wrote the Royal College exams. However, by the time I encountered the problem with failing the second part (oral), I had committed to going to St. Anthony for a year beginning in July 1964. I wanted to experience work and living there as a general pediatrician to decide if I should stay a generalist or complete training as a subspecialist in pediatric cardiology.

My years of training at the Montreal Children's Hospital were some of the happiest of my life before marriage. During this time, my sister Millie graduated in nursing from the St. John's General Hospital, and I was privileged to return to Newfoundland for her graduation and share the happy occasion with several other relatives. Aunt Josie and her husband came from Eastport; Aunt Alma came from St. Anthony and Aunt Bertha came from Flower's Cove. Other family members attended from St. John's, including Aunt Ella Spurrell (sister to Grandfather Way), her son Pearce who was an internist in the city, and her son Roland who was an executive with the mining company in Baie Verte. Following graduation Millie and her classmate, Doris Tucker, came and worked at the Montreal Children's Hospital. It was the first time we were able to enjoy each other's company as adults. They rented an apartment in a cul-de-sac close to the hospital so Betty and I would often drop in for a visit when we were out in the car.

During my final months at the Montreal Children's Hospital, I befriended Dr. Martin Lees, who had accepted to become head of pediatric cardiology at the University of Oregon Medical Centre, Portland, and he invited me to join him if I decided to take further subspecialty training in cardiology.

CHAPTER 20

Romance And Marriage

July 1961- December 1963

I visited with Betty at her home on my first evening back from Vancouver. We chatted with her parents for a time and then they retired to allow us some privacy. We were sitting close at one end of their sofa, in subdued light, and chatting about all that had transpired over the previous year. Something in the corner of the seat started bothering my left elbow, so I put my hand down to explore the area. A strange object greeted my hand which, on closer inspection, was a set of dentures. We broke into convulsive laughter, and her parents upstairs heard our hilarity, and couldn't resist inquiring what was so funny. Mother was embarrassed but came down to laugh with us and recovered her teeth.

After settling back at the Montreal Children's, I began to visit the Milne home regularly and also attend Snowdon Baptist Church. Betty was into her training as a nurse at the Montreal General Hospital. Our schedules were not well meshed as regards free time, but we were usually available on weekends. So we saw each other on Sundays at church, and Mrs. Milne always seemed keen to invite me back to their home for lunch. There is a saying, 'the way to a man's heart is through his stomach', and her cooking certainly helped me along. Betty's brother claimed that his mother was just taking pity on a poor orphan boy who had no family in Montreal and was obviously lonely. As Betty and I saw each other more often and up close, the bond between us grew stronger, so our relationship progressed over the next two years. I had a car so we could get out and be alone some evenings to have discussions about our relationship and its future.

The relationship was not without its tensions and rough spots. Betty felt drawn to the mission field, and it took some persuasion to convince her that St. Anthony was also a mission field. When we were serious to the point of buying an engagement ring I, jokingly, offered to give the $500.00 (a lot of money in 1963) to a mission of her choice rather than purchase the ring. Fortunately, she balked at this suggestion and accepted the ring when I formally proposed marriage.

The cul-de-sac where my sister lived became a favorite parking spot for Betty and me, whenever we were out in the car. On one occasion it was the location of a breakup between us. I don't remember what the issue was, but it looked like our relationship was over. We did not contact each other for several weeks by which time both of us were bursting with misery and loneliness. Eventually, I screwed up my courage and called her and told her how I felt and that I was sorry. She indicated similar feelings, and we agreed to get back together. From that time on, our relationship flourished, and we both knew we could not do without each other.

While this was happening, I had to keep focused on my studies in preparation for the Fellowship exams in Pediatrics. I was under some stress as summer, 1963, approached. Betty and I became engaged in late spring and scheduled marriage for the end of December. Betty's graduation in nursing also happened a few weeks earlier, so I tried for an opportunity to visit Mr. Milne alone, to get his consent, but found it difficult to work out. I devised what I thought was a clever scheme. Betty's mom always attended church on Sunday mornings, and Mr. Milne stayed home. I decided, on a bright sunny Sunday, to take a chance that this situation would prove accurate and drove to their home on Trenholme Avenue. Everything looked clear as I approached the house. Mr. Milne's car was in the driveway, so I bravely rang the doorbell and waited. After a short pause, the door opened and, Mrs. Milne appeared in her housecoat and curlers. She was not feeling well that Sunday! In any event, I was invited in and, with few preliminaries, I explained the purpose of my visit to both of them and they gladly consented to the plan.

I bought an engagement ring and carried it in my coat pocket for a couple of weeks until the opportunity seemed right to propose formally. When the moment came, Betty graciously accepted. After some discussion, we selected December 28, 1963, as the day for our wedding. The date was convenient as we had holidays available for a short honeymoon and it did not clash with the schedule for the Royal College Fellowship exams.

On the Friday night, before the ceremony, there was the usual rehearsal at the church. This event was rather unnerving to me as I had to repeat my vows three times and I went back to my room at the hospital and hardly slept a wink. Next morning, I went to the cafeteria, as I normally did, and sat across from a fellow trainee who happened to be the resident in psychiatry. I told him my predicament about my lack of sleep and what was taking place in my life later that day. He said he could help me get through the wedding ceremony without too much emotional stress and gave me some tablets – largactil, a tranquilizer – to help me. About an hour or so before the ceremony I took my pills as prescribed, as did my best man, Dale, who was also nervous. Both of us did fine except that a side effect of the medication was to give us dry eyes that felt full of sand and we could hardly keep them open for the church ceremony and the several hours it took for the reception, dinner, and speeches. Nevertheless, we made it through. The ceremony took place at Snowden Baptist Church and was conducted by Rev. Ellerd Corbett. The reception took place at the Airport Hilton Hotel so that we would be close to the airport for an evening flight. Most of Betty's family were in attendance. The Munkittricks came to represent my family, with Dale serving as best man and his wife, Annabelle, as an attendant. After the speeches and a lovely dinner, the waiters turned off the lights and marched around the room with slabs of Baked Alaska mounted with sparklers. Everyone was delighted by this glittering finale.

31. After the ceremony, December 28, 1963

After the festivities, we changed to traveling clothes and caught a plane to New York City for the night. We arrived at the hotel and went to the restaurant for refreshments. The place had many young couples wearing corsages and obviously, like us, having their first night of marriage. Next morning, we caught a plane to Tampa and spent the following week at Clearwater Beach. Ironically, we stayed at the Mount Royal Motel which was comfortable and had a nice pool. But the weather was very cool and not conducive to swimming. Nevertheless, we had a good week together unwinding from work and the stress of the ceremony. We returned to Montreal to our new home – a rented flat in Snowdon very near the church. The owner was a widow who spent time in Florida with her children. She allowed us to have her furnished place for six months – an ideal arrangement as we were going to St. Anthony in July. We were very comfortable, and my only concern was a lovely white brocade sofa which I feared would get soiled and ruined during our stay. Betty settled into housekeeping and working as a nurse at the Montreal General Hospital. She often entertained on weekends, especially her parents and aunts, and her favorite desert for a time was cheesecake. I gained several extra pounds even though the stress of work and exams continued with me into the spring of 1964.

As June approached, we began to plan for the adventure of spending a year at St. Anthony, where I would serve on staff as a doctor, and Betty would be a nurse. I would be able to introduce Betty to my family at Flower's Cove and life in Newfoundland. Naturally, I was looking forward to being close to my relatives again, especially my sister who had returned to St. Anthony as a nurse at the hospital.

CHAPTER 21

Our Year In St. Anthony

(JULY 1964 - JUNE 1965)

We arrived in St. Anthony around July 1st, 1964, to begin our time as part of the medical staff at the Grenfell Mission Hospital. Betty worked as a nurse in the Sanatorium, and I served as one of the general physicians. I had particular responsibility for the pediatric ward and children in the outpatient clinic, but I also covered the medical needs of the adult wards and Sanatorium, especially when my colleague, Dr. John Gray, was away. In addition to Dr. Gray, the staff included Dr. Walter Spitzer, who was a general surgeon and his wife Mary, who was an ophthalmologist. Dr. Alasdair Smith was in charge of the outpatient clinic and emergency. Dr. John Cronhelm was the anesthetist, and Dr. Gordon Thomas was the senior surgeon. Dr. Herbert Bowles was obstetrician/gynecologist. Dr. Jim Williams was the pathologist in charge of laboratory services. My sister was in charge of the pediatric ward, and her future sister-in-law was the head nurse in the operating room. Other relatives worked at the hospital in various support services.

Betty and I were given a large room on the second floor of Grenfell House as our living quarters. Grenfell House was built by local men for Dr. Grenfell and his bride after their marriage in 1919, and it was their home for all of their life together in St. Anthony. The room was probably the master bedroom when Dr. Grenfell lived there. We could eat breakfast with the staff living there, or go to the cafeteria in the hospital. After a month or so we were moved to *The Bungalow* as our home for the balance of the year. This small cottage style home is set back in the woods on the hillside behind the hospital and close to Grenfell House. One of its outstanding features was its heating system. It had a wood burning fireplace and a supply of firewood in an attached shed. However, for winter heating, it had radiators which were fed steam through pipes connected to a steam plant about three blocks away. All of the mission buildings and homes received heat through this system. When steam began to arrive in the radiators, there would be loud cracking and bangs as the steam expanded the pipes and radiators. The home was ideal for us, secluded by woods, very private and comfortable. It had two bedrooms in the back, separated by a bathroom which served both bedrooms. There was a kitchen area with separate entrance. The large front room and dining area overlooked the hospital and harbor, with a lovely view through a bay window that had small trees growing around it. But there was one problem. We regularly saw mice in the wood shed and kitchen area, and this was a bit uncomfortable for both of us, thinking they might invade our living area and bedroom.

Shortly after we got settled, we realized that Betty might be pregnant. We were very excited when this was confirmed. Nevertheless, she would continue to work on the wards until a few weeks before her delivery in March 1965.

In November 1964, we were treated to a visit from Bob and Ruth Hill. Bob was Dr. Arthur Hill's son and one of the young men who met me at the bus when I arrived in Sherbrooke in 1949. He was an employee of Canadian National Railway so they took the train from Sherbrooke to Sydney, NS, then the ferry across the Cabot Strait to Port aux Basque, and the 'Newfie Bullet' train to Corner Brook. Betty and I drove down the gravel road from St. Anthony to meet them. We got back as far as Daniel's Harbour and chose to stay at the new motel for the night. After we had arrived, we decided to have a meal at the small restaurant operated by the motel owner. The restaurant overlooked the ocean and was part of a general store and gas station separate from the accommodation. We sat in a booth and waited patiently for service. Eventually, a young waitress came to take our orders. Bob ordered a cheeseburger. She asked him what a cheeseburger was, and he explained it was a hamburger with cheese on top. Sure enough, when our orders arrived, Bob's sandwich had a slice of cheese on top of the bun. We kept our composure until she had returned to the kitchen. Bob was a big overweight guy with a rubber face and comical eyes and when he lifted his eyes to meet mine all four of us began to shake with laughter and had trouble getting control of ourselves. It was okay that the rest of them should laugh convulsively, but I was known to the staff as the famous and dignified doctor from St. Anthony. After the meal, we retired to our adjacent motel rooms. Soon, Betty and I could hear Bob and Ruth laughing in their unit just as the lights went out for the night around 9:00 in the evening when the generator got turned off. I think they had a flashlight, but their laughter occurred when Bob flushed the toilet, and everything came up in the bathtub. The motel was brand new, and apparently, the plumbing had not been thoroughly tested. Next day we slowly made our way over the bumpy - and sometimes boggy - road back to St. Anthony. Once we were settled back at our bungalow, Bob and Ruth had a relaxing week by the fireplace keeping the wood burning to neutralize the November chill while Betty and I spent our days at the hospital. During their week with us, my sister Millie was married to Bill Simms. Bob sang at the wedding, and I know that all of the local folks appreciated his voice. After the week, we took them back down over the road to Corner Brook to catch the train to Port aux Basque, the ferry for Sydney, and the train back to Sherbrooke.

The cheeseburger incident was the source for a good laugh the next several summers when we met for holidays at Lake Wallace. One following summer we were visiting Bob and Ruth at their cottage, and I began reading an issue of *Time* magazine. It had a picture of a prominent actress dressed in a revealing swimsuit. We were kidding around, and someone suggested I paint the picture as a Christmas gift for Bob. "Good enough," says I (as we Newfies would say) and tucked the idea away as something I would do as a surprise. For several summers, Betty and I had attended a painting class conducted by Roy Langley, a respected local artist and good friend from Grace Chapel, so oil painting was something I did as a hobby for stress relief.

After getting back to St. John's I spent time in my basement working on the oil painting for Bob's Christmas gift. At one point the fumes from the paint set off the fire alarm, and Betty kidded me about the 'hot' picture. We packaged it and sent it off in time for Christmas. The next summer we returned and visited Bob's cottage to see the painting, which he had mounted on the inside of the bathroom door so when you sat on the 'throne,' the painting was unavoidably in your line of vision. We enjoyed a good laugh every time we visited for several more summers until they sold the cottage and contents. I don't know what happened to my valuable painting, but it became the property of a prominent sportsperson who subsequently became a Canadian Senator, so it may well be hanging in a mansion in the nation's capital and bringing chuckles there.

My life as a doctor at St. Anthony was busy. In short order, I found myself filling more than the role of pediatrician and general medical consultant. There were times when Dr. Thomas and Dr. Gray were both away, so I was asked to approve air ambulance flights and handle other administrative duties. I worked closely with Dr. Smith in the outpatient area and with Dr. John Cronhelm in the intensive care. Dr. Cronhelm was a gifted anesthetist and highly regarded by the surgical team and respected by the medical staff for his ability to help in medical crises. For me, being inexperienced and new, it was reassuring to be able to call on him at any time of the day for help in a difficult situation. He had a clear analytical approach to problems which invariably led to improving the situation. Dr. Alisdair Smith was a typical conservative British doctor with excellent clinical skills. He frequently traveled to do clinics at the nursing stations.

Dr. John Gray trained in England and was an outstanding Internist. He was very knowledgeable and empathetic, with an excellent bedside manner that endeared him to the local people, especially the elderly. Subsequently, after 25 years of faithful service, he left St. Anthony and joined the Faculty of Medicine at Dalhousie University as Professor of Geriatric Medicine. A Center for Geriatric Care was built at St. Anthony a few years later and named in his honor. This recognition was much-deserved for his years of service to the people of Northern Newfoundland and Labrador.

Dr. Gordon Thomas was not only the senior surgeon, and superintendent, but the dynamo behind modernization of the Medical Services in the region. He was a 'Type A' person; a man of few words but decisive and all action. He was very skilled as a surgeon and kept himself up-to-date by going for specialty training throughout his career, including extra training in thoracic surgery, so he could do thoracoplasty (partial removal of ribs to allow collapse (rest) of part of the underlying lung). This operation was very helpful in patients with tuberculosis and helped control the advance of this disease. He trained in Cardiovascular Surgery and wanted to do heart valve surgery in St. Anthony. The medical, anesthesia and nursing staff who would have to support him with post-operative intensive care considered this beyond their level of competence and resisted the plan. Some tension arose over this as Dr. Thomas was not a man to easily accept 'no' for an answer. However, after due consideration, he accepted reality and did not proceed with this venture. He was an active administrator and often irritated the International Grenfell Association Board by asking them to 'rubber stamp' decisions he had made, and acted on, months before they met for their annual meeting. The Board included several prominent Grenfell Mission alumni who had become bankers, lawyers, and physicians in New York

32. Dr. Gordon W. Thomas.

and Boston and were not accustomed to being 'rubber stamps'. I was privileged to be a Board member for several years and witnessed some of this. Despite limited resources Dr. Thomas bulldozed medical services from dogsled and hospital ship days to aircraft and ambulance, taking advantage of the roads and airstrips that finally arrived in the area in the 1960s.

Dr. Thomas was a special person to me because he had persuaded Mrs. Curtis to fund my education at Sherbrooke High School and Bishop's University. Working at his home was an important part of my teenage years, and Mrs. Thomas was an excellent conversationalist who always took an interest in me when I was at their house. Dr. Thomas became a father figure to me when I was completing my training and deciding my future. Although we corresponded seldom and he was a man of few words, I always knew he was there for me if I had any problems. Unfortunately, his retirement years in Nova Scotia were cut short when an interventional procedure for coronary artery disease resulted in complications and death.

As we got into the fall of 1964 Betty was feeling her pregnancy, and this limited my travel to see patients. I did several small clinics to nearby places like Flower's Cove and Bird Cove. I made one medical trip to Labrador with stops in Forteau, Mary's Harbour, Cartwright, and Happy Valley. During the early winter, I had one scary flight to Cartwright for a clinic. I sat in the co-pilot seat with Ron Penney at the controls of the old Norseman. When we lifted off from the St. Anthony airstrip, we saw the Strait of Belle Isle's open water with scattered patches of ice and whitecaps. It was foreboding to think what would happen if our single engine failed. Soon we reached the mainland of Labrador but bucking a moderate headwind which was slowing our progress. Then we encountered a snow squall and had to fly through a whiteout. Pilot Ron was in radio contact with Cartwright and was informed the weather was clear there, so he decided to continue north. Eventually, we broke through the falling snow and had clear visibility as we approached our destination, but the experience was very sobering to me. I will always admire the bush pilots who risk their lives regularly to fly in the weather conditions of Labrador and the Canadian Arctic.

We had a wonderful Christmas season with visits to various staff homes, and we hosted a party for several hospital workers that had become friends. We spent family time at the home of Aunt Alma and Uncle Lester Penney. They had two young children which enlivened our visit but, more importantly, we always played Rook as evening entertainment. Uncle Les was a character and loved to upset Aunt Alma by pretending to cheat or give signals to his partner, who was always me. It was a lot of fun, and we always had a cup of tea and lunch at the end of the game. We introduced Aunt Alma to Blue Cheese or 'stinky' cheese. That was something most Newfoundlanders would never eat at that time, but once she got the taste we had it regularly on toast as part of our lunch. After the New Year celebration (1965) we continued our weekly visits for Rook at Aunt Alma's even though Betty was into her final trimester of pregnancy. Some nights became stormy with drifting snow which made the short drive somewhat tricky.

Early in 1965, I was scheduled to do a winter clinic with Miss Cree, who was the nurse stationed at Cartwright in Labrador. This trip required traveling by snowmobile from Cartwright to Mary's Harbour, with stops in the small communities along the way to conduct clinics and stay overnight. I did not relish making this journey especially as Betty was nearing delivery. Fortunately, a severe winter storm canceled everything, so I never got to experience snowmobiling in Labrador.

In March 1965 Betty's mom and dad arrived from Montreal just a day before our son, Gregory, was born. They flew to Gander, and the mission plane brought them north to St. Anthony. The birth went smoothly, and both

Betty's parents, Jessie and George Milne

mother and child did well. Dr. Herbert Bowles supervised the delivery. He was a retired Professor of Obstetrics from the University of Hawaii, who was resident Obstetrician for the year. During Betty's stay in the hospital we had one of the worst snowfalls on record, and when she left to walk the short distance to the bungalow, the snowdrift was about two stories high. Consequently, we had some difficulty getting her and baby back home. But the snow made things very cozy and beautiful when the weather cleared. Betty's parents stayed for about a week and then the mission plane took them back to Gander for their return to Montreal.

Like all new parents, we were nervous about the baby and the possibility he might stop breathing in the night. Initially, we kept him in a crib in our room and at night I would frequently use a flashlight to check that all was well. We were also anxious about the presence of mice around the bungalow and worried that one might get into his crib and bite him. In fact, we got a real scare a couple of weeks later. After Betty's parents had gone home, the extra bedroom was free, and we decided to move baby there and keep the bathroom doors open on both sides so we could hear him. About 2:00 AM he let out a scream and scared both of us. I jumped out of bed and ran to check on him with my flashlight. However, he was sound asleep and settled as if nothing had happened. I went back to bed but had difficulty getting any rest. Just as every obstetrician should have a baby, so every pediatrician should have a child to learn the basics of infant care and feeding. I learned more general pediatrics after Gregory was born than during my three years of specialty training. He was a 'blurper' (prone to projectile regurgitations) during feeds so feeding times were challenging and I got several baths with carnation milk.

Betty and I were active in the ministry of the United Church during our year. We sang in the choir and participated in Bible studies. On Sunday evenings, it was customary to have a short hymn sing and devotional in the hospital chapel which was shared over the public address system with the patients throughout the wards. I participated in this and took my turn at bringing a short devotional when requested.

As spring approached, I had to decide what to do regarding our future. I could have stayed at St. Anthony and chosen to remain a general pediatrician rather than continue my specialization in pediatric cardiology. After much deliberation, I felt I should not waste my year of training in cardiology but should return to an academic center and complete training as a subspecialist. I decided to accept the invitation of Dr. Lees to join him for a two-year fellowship in Pediatric Cardiology at The University of Oregon Medical Centre. During this time, I would also make another attempt to secure my fellowship in pediatrics. In the 1960's, The University of Oregon was one of the leading centers in Cardiac Surgery and invasive catheter procedures. Dr. Albert Starr was their Chief of Cardiac Surgery, and he was one of the first to use an artificial valve in the heart. Also, Dr. Charles Dotter and Dr. Mel Judkins were pioneering the procedures - that are now routine - for unblocking cardiac and peripheral arteries through the use of catheter dilations.

My decision meant that I would have to become an immigrant to the USA, which was a requirement for acceptance into the training program. I completed Immigration and medical forms for the three of us. In the late spring, we flew to St. John's for medical exams, X-rays, and a visit to the US consulate. For our medicals, we visited Dr. Fraser, a very elderly practitioner who was operating out of a Norman Rockwell style office. We passed the medicals and got approved for immigration; all of which we found rather amusing.

The Newfoundland Medical Association was holding its annual meeting while we were in the city. Therefore, we took advantage and attended their social function at the Crow's Nest, a popular watering hole for the 'townies'. I sampled some smoked salmon – supposedly a delicacy – which made me desperately sick a few hours later and I have never touched the stuff since.

I met several pediatricians and medical leaders during our visit, including Dr. Cluny McPherson, registrar of the Medical Association, and Dr. Leonard Miller, Deputy Minister of Health. I also met Dr. Cliff Joy for the first time. He was a Boston and Montreal trained pediatrician, and also a member of the Provincial Legislature with an inside track to Premier Joey Smallwood. He was lobbying Joey to establish a Children's Hospital in St. John's.

The creation of a separate and independent Children's Hospital was a controversial medical-political issue in the mid-1900. The few models that existed were in major population centers – Boston, Montreal, Toronto, and Halifax. All of them had their roots in charitable organizations, often nursing led, and initially aimed at helping low-income families treat their children during infectious disease epidemics. These epidemics killed many infants and youth before the end of World War Two when antibiotics arrived as a treatment for many common infections. Dr. Joy's models were in Boston and Montreal where he had trained and where pediatric care and teaching was among the best in the world.

When he returned to St. John's to practice, there was a division of pediatric facilities between three hospitals and an infectious disease unit, attached to the General Hospital, known as *The Fever*. The latter specialized in isolating and treating contagious patients and the facility occupied an old building with woefully inadequate space and equipment. The government and the medical profession were both embarrassed by this situation so Dr. Joy had a fertile field in which to lobby for a dedicated children's hospital. His primary opponents were the established hospitals that did not want to give up pediatric facilities and, to some extent, the government, which considered such an undertaking far too expensive.

The hospital at Fort Pepperell, the former US Military base in the east end of St. John's, had been closed and abandoned for some years. But, the property was up for grabs, and there was political jockeying to have it reactivated and made into a Children's Orthopedic and Rehabilitation Center (led by Dr. Ted Shapter) or a Children's Hospital (led by Dr. Cliff Joy). Later, while I was in Oregon, the decision was made (influenced by Dr. Joy) to have Dr. Charles Janeway, Chief Pediatrician at the Boston Children's Hospital, come to St. John's and adjudicate between the two choices. Dr. Janeway told Premier Smallwood that the choice should be a Children's Hospital and he agreed to have his name attached to the new center. Premier Smallwood, in typically flamboyant style, made the grand announcement and said the hospital would be called 'The Dr. Charles A. Janeway Child Health Centre'. The Premier, reportedly, was later to observe that he spent three million dollars without gaining a single vote.

The old building at Fort Pepperell was both hospital and bomb shelter for the military base, so the lower level was built partly into the side of the adjacent hill, with extra thick walls, which made renovations and alterations challenging and expensive. After the Americans had left the base, looting took place so that even the doors were missing. By mid-1966, repairs and restoration were complete, and Dr. Janeway's name appeared on the side of the building. However, the name was soon shortened to 'The Janeway Child Health Centre', or just 'The Janeway.' The people of the Province rapidly recognized it as a first class facility for treatment of their sick children. I was half way through my training in Oregon and had no idea that a year later I would be returning to Newfoundland as a staff physician at this new facility. As I write this, plans are being made to celebrate the fiftieth anniversary of *The Janeway* in September 2016.

Early in June 1965, we prepared to leave St. Anthony. It had been a fantastic year for us and the experience I gained strengthened me for my future administrative roles. On the morning we left, we were waiting on the steps of the hospital for our ride to the airstrip when a bulldozer drove into the field in front of us and started digging a hole. The excavation was the start of a large modern medical facility for St. Anthony which was named *The Dr. Charles S. Curtis Hospital* and today it stands as a fitting memorial to Dr. Grenfell's successor as surgeon and Mission Superintendent.

CHAPTER 22

The Oregon Years

(JULY 1965 – JUNE 1967)

THE LONG JOURNEY WEST TO Oregon was broken by a short stay in Montreal to visit with Betty's parents. Gregory was only three months old but alert enough to know things were changing. The mission plane took us to St. John's. For the flight to Montreal, we had arranged for Air Canada to supply us with a 'sky cot' for the baby, thinking he would sleep peacefully for most of the trip. This contraption was a basket that attached to the luggage compartment above our heads. However, he decided he was having nothing to do with this arrangement and screamed blue murder every time we tried to settle him in the cot. So we had to abandon the plan and allow him to sleep in mother's arms. After our time in Montreal, we flew to Portland without further trouble. When we arrived, we were welcomed by Dr. Lees and his family, who had us stay with them for a couple of nights while we searched for an apartment. We found housing close to the University too expensive for our budget and went west to Beaverton, ten miles from our new workplace where we found a townhouse that met our needs. We signed in and proceeded to scout out sources for used furniture. Finding things to meet our needs was not too difficult. We sought out a church and settled on Allan Avenue Baptist located in a small building across town. The people were very friendly and helpful in getting us settled, and we soon felt at home.

One of my first tasks was to buy a car. Our new friends at church directed us to the Ford dealership, and I bought a Fairlane and proceeded to drive it to the licensing bureau to obtain plates and a driver's license. When parking in front of the office I noticed that the car next to me was about to back out. The driver was a teenage girl. In the passenger seat was a uniformed male with a clipboard in hand which told me she was about to take her driver's test. She proceeded to back out and turned sharply clipping the rear end of my new car and ripping off the bumper. Needless to say, there was a moment of immense shock for myself and her. The instructor directed her to move forward and park, following which he got out and inspected the damage and collected some vital information. The Ford dealership was very kind and repaired the car for me, but it meant being without my personal wheels for a couple of extra days.

It was a couple more days before we settled everything and I could begin work at the hospital. The Dornbecker Children's unit, where I would work, occupied a full floor of the University Medical Center. The environment was very similar to what I had known in Montreal with a lot of friendly and helpful people. Dr. Olmstead was Chief of Pediatrics, and he was very welcoming. In addition to Dr. Lees in cardiology, there was an Aussie fellow, Dr. Harry Burnell from Adelaide, who shared clinical duties with me on the cardiology service. The three of us shared a long narrow office room with standard desks and telephone service. There was no privacy space, and we had to talk quietly so as not to disturb Dr. Lees, who was very focused on his research interests. There was a research lab for us in a building across the street, and I was expected, with the help of a lab technician, to work on a project which Dr. Lees had started. Our clinics for outpatients occurred in The Crippled Children's unit in another building. The clinic supervisor was Dr. Victor Menashe, a cordial general pediatrician with training and skills in cardiology. Harry and I worked out a schedule for on-call coverage, work at the outpatient clinic and cardiac catheterization lab work. We attended conferences and presented patients to the surgeons for surgical procedures when needed. I tried to make some progress with the research project but found the sampling methods much too tedious for consistent results, even on samples from the same source. The analysis of samples involved gas chromatography, a new technique at the time, which neither the technician nor I fully understood. Jumping ahead here in my story, I should say that after working intermittently for the two years, we had little to show in the way of reliable results although Dr. Lees did manage to get a publication or two out of our efforts.

After a few months, Betty and I relocated to a townhouse near the church and closer to some of our new friends. The move provided Betty and Gregory more company while I was at work. Our new address was 'Why Worry Lane' and we occupied a spacious unit with three bedrooms that allowed us to have visitors, particularly Betty's parents. We became more involved in the life of Allan Avenue Baptist Church, and it was wonderful to feel again at home in a church family. They were outgrowing their small building and began a new sanctuary attached to the original building. We were there when they moved to the new Worship Center, and we noted the dramatic effect it had on the people. The coziness was gone, and the singing sounded dead in the large vaulted space, and this changed the whole atmosphere of church life. We had the privilege of going back for a visit about thirty years later and were sad to note that they never recovered from the change, and their membership stopped growing. The building looked almost as new and unused as the day they moved in. We enjoyed a wonderful reunion and hospitality in the home of Dean and Janice Johnson, who were still attending the church, but their reports, sadly, indicated the original congregation had failed to reproduce itself spiritually, and two small ethnic churches are now renting the building.

In the fall of 1965, I traveled to Ottawa for my second attempt at the fellowship exam and was successful. It was a great relief to get this behind me. During the fall, we also visited with Dr. Herbert Bowles, the obstetrician from St. Anthony, who was now living in retirement at Lake Chelan, Washington. We took a ferry from the east end of the long lake as there was no road into the small resort community where he lived. He had built a beautiful log cabin, near the lake's west end, in a valley at the foot of a mountain. In the fall morning, with all of the colored leaves around, and tame deer wandering into his back area, it was a most beautiful experience. We also visited with my cousin Roland Kean, and his wife Angela, at Moses Lake, Washington. They were stationed there in the American armed forces.

Our second child, Caroline, was born in July 1966 at the start of our second year in Oregon. The pregnancy and delivery went well but the subsequent night was miserable for Betty, who shared a room with a very unsettled woman. Fortunately, the next day we negotiated Betty's early discharge home. The following morning we drove to Twin Rocks on the Oregon coast for a wonderful holiday week. Gregory was fifteen months, and he and I enjoyed our time together at the beach while Betty and Caroline rested in the shelter of some driftwood or back at the motel.

During our final year in Oregon, we were preoccupied with where to settle for practice. The choice seemed to be Vancouver or back to Newfoundland. About midway through the year, I was contacted by Dr. Dennis Vince in Vancouver about joining him in pediatric cardiology at the children's hospital. I knew Dr. Vince from my year (1960-61) of pediatric training in Vancouver. We had talked at subsequent medical meetings, and he had expressed interest in having me join him at the end of my training. In the spring of 1967, I accepted his invitation to come and look at the economics of living in Vancouver and operating a private office. I discovered I would be ten thousand dollars in debt before I saw my first patient, not including the costs of moving and finding a home for my family. This potential debt worried and scared me considerably as I was aware other young pediatric cardiologists were struggling in Vancouver due to a lack of investigative facilities and hospital beds. Dr. Vince kept reassuring me not to worry as he would direct patients my way until I had a secure practice. I decided to seek counsel from Dr. Thomas back in St. Anthony and Dr. Cliff Joy at the new Janeway Child Health Centre in St. John's. Both were very helpful, especially Dr. Joy, who wanted me to return to St. John's even though Dr. John Collins was there and overseeing the development of a Pediatric Cardiology service. Dr. Joy said he could get me a retainer at the Janeway, which would help me get established if I returned there. I was offered living space in a new apartment building owned by the hospital for our first accommodation as this would also be a financial help and enable us to take the time to identify permanent housing. I was attracted to this proposal as it gave me an opportunity to return to Newfoundland. Second, it would be an opportunity to serve the whole island including the Grenfell Mission hospitals in St. Anthony and Labrador. Third, there was the prospect of becoming part of a new medical school in St. John's, something that was under active exploration at that time, and these things were very persuasive.

I was torn emotionally about reneging on my commitment to Dr. Vince but, after considerable deliberation, I made the decision to return to Newfoundland. Dr. Vince was very gracious about my reversal and said he would be glad to have me come to Vancouver if things did not work out in St. John's. I informed Dr. Thomas, and he wrote me a very kind personal letter expressing happiness at my return to 'the rock' even though I would not be based at St. Anthony. Dr. Joy was thrilled and bent over backward to work out all the details at the hospital and with the Newfoundland Medical Association.

As we came to the end of our time in Oregon, we had mixed feelings. We loved Oregon and were well received during our time there. We had made many friends in the medical center and at Allen Avenue Baptist Church. I probably could have stayed but, being a landed immigrant and draft eligible, with the Viet Nam War in full swing, I felt I should get back to Canada before they discovered me.

I shall never forget our last day in Oregon. We had spent the previous week packing and scheduling everything. Betty and the children were to fly to Montreal and stay with her parents while I drove the car and a trailer across the country to catch up with them. In the morning, after cleanup and the finishing touches to packing, I drove Betty and the children to the Portland Airport and saw them leave on their journey to Montreal. I returned to our empty apartment and experienced one of the loneliest moments I ever experienced in my life. I wept as I thought about my family about to be three thousand miles away and I had to drive, towing a loaded trailer, all that distance before we could be together again. With the help of a friend from the church I crammed some of the remaining boxes into the car. The trailer was full and secured with a tarpaulin in place. At the last minute, I had to lash some boxes to the roof rack of the car. After a prayer together and some tears as we parted, I was off on my journey.

All went well for about the first hour. I was now driving along the Columbia River Highway on the south side of the Columbia Gorge. This area experiences severe wind gusts which, without warning, can dislodge roof rack items. Suddenly, a gust lifted two of the boxes off the car roof, and they sailed over the trailer and landed on the pavement. Fortunately, they rolled off to the side of the road avoiding the oncoming cars behind me. I stopped on the shoulder as fast as I could and, after gathering my wits, went back to inspect the boxes and pick them up. I found space in the car for both boxes but began to cry because I recognized that one contained our best china which was a wedding gift from Betty's parents. I was in dread of the moment when Betty would open it and discover the damage. I guess I informed her by phone when I stopped for the night, but that did not relieve my anxiety.

Later that same day another crisis arose. It was sunny and hot, and my car engine was pulling a loaded vehicle, plus the heavy trailer, up the western slope of the Great Divide, and I noticed that the engine's temperature gauge was starting to climb. As I got to within a mile of the summit, the engine began to chug and lose power. There was no shoulder or place to pull over and allow the motor to cool. With much caution, I nursed the car to the top and, with great relief, started to coast down the eastern slope and into Montana. At the bottom, there was a small community with a gas station at the traffic light. I pulled into the station as the car engine stalled and I thought the worst had happened. I explained events to the attendant, and he lifted the hood to inspect things. After a few minutes, he said 'try her now.' I turned the ignition switch, and the motor started and sounded normal. He smiled at me and said 'the wire came off one of your spark plugs.' I smiled back at him as he said there was no charge, and I silently said a thank you to the Lord above. I filled up at the station, and used the bathroom, before continuing on my way. The next 1000 miles or so were comfortable driving as I crossed the flatlands of Montana and the Dakotas. I was able to arrive in Montreal without further incident and ahead of schedule.

In Montreal, we rested for a few days and showed off our beautiful children to various relatives that Mom and Dad Milne insisted we visit or had over for tea. The day after my arrival we bravely opened the boxes that had blown off the car roof. Much to my relief, the only damage in the box of china was a handle broken off one teacup. The damaged cup was easily repairable with some glue, or replaceable. We juggled our load to make room in the car for Betty and the two children for the drive to Newfoundland.

After our rest days, the four of us boarded the car and drove east to the ferry in Sydney, NS, with an overnight stop in Edmundston, N.B.: We had a good trip and crossed over to Argentia without incident. After a one-and-a-half hour drive we were in St. John's and heading to the east end to find our apartment adjacent to the Janeway Hospital. We secured our keys from the caretaker and proceeded to unpack and set up our belongings. The apartment was bright and adequate for our family at the time. Also, it was only a five-minute walk down the hill to my work.

34. The Janeway as I knew it.

CHAPTER 23

My First Days At The Janeway

(July 1967)

After the July 1st weekend, I met with Dr. Joy at the hospital, and he introduced me to Mr. Kelland and the other administrative staff. The hospital had been open just a year and was still struggling with staffing and administrative issues. I was shown to my office on the second floor, a large impressive corner suite with large windows in the two outside walls, a grand polished desk, and private bathroom. It was the biggest office in the building. A year earlier it had been occupied by medical consultants from England who had been brought in on a short-term basis to oversee the selection of medical staff, formation of a Medical Advisory Committee and other administrative structures. In those years, Newfoundland's political leadership tended not to trust local experts as advisors, choosing instead to import external consultants. The outsiders flew in for a week or so, sat and listened to local specialists and copied down everything they said. Then, they flew home and produced a stunning report with recommendations – all of which had been voiced by the locals – and accompanied their document with a hefty fee.

Dr. Joy occupied an office next door and Dr. Kennedy, Chief of Surgery, would have the third space when he recovered from his heart attack. There was an adjacent area for secretaries, and one of the ladies would work for me. The setup tended to give one a 'swelled head' except that, in my case, I was the junior member of staff, an administrative 'greenhorn' apart from experience as Chief Resident at the Montreal Children's Hospital and occasionally delegated roles at St. Anthony. But, and this was a big BUT, I was the only pediatrician on staff with a Fellowship from The Royal College of Physicians of Canada and, for some reason, this was thought to convey superior administrative powers. At this point, I had no administrative responsibilities except to assist Dr. Joy in patient care and bed occupancy management.

It was summertime, so the patient care units (wards) were quiet; only those patients clearly in need of attention were present in the house. With school out and easy travel, patients from the out ports were booked for elective surgery, so there was a greater need for surgical beds. Even beds on the medical wards were being utilized for surgery patients so Dr. Joy and I had to make sure we had enough beds available to serve the needs of the emergency clinic.

I soon discovered that being based at the hospital meant a longer week. Dr. Joy tended to do morning rounds seven days a week to assist the staff with finding beds as needed. Since he was Chief of Staff, he often exercised his authority to discharge patients under the care of other physicians. Often patients with homes nearby could be discharged safely. I tended to come in on Saturday mornings, to be available to the nursing staff, especially when Dr. Joy could not be there. We had a few trainees on rotation as interns, and they and the nurses always found it helpful to have a staff physician available to assist with inpatient problems.

On my second day on the job, I explored the big office. A Dictaphone was on the desk with some spare tapes. I decided to investigate what was recorded on the tapes so as not to destroy any recordings of importance. The first tape I checked contained a dictation by Dr. Kennedy. I had met him previously and immediately recognized his unique Harbor Main Irish/Newfie brogue. During the first winter and spring after the hospital opened there had been a problem with lack of heat in the operating rooms. No solution could be found to this dilemma until one day, in a fit of rage, Dr. Kennedy grabbed the thermostat on the wall and yanked it off, only to discover its connection was to - NOTHING! Still fuming, he had gone to his office and dictated an appropriate memo to the Administrator. As I listened to him dictating his emotional message, the humor of it brought on a fit of convulsive laughter that remained with me for days whenever I remembered the recording. Needless to say, I did not erase it and hope his transcribed message might still be in the hospital archives. No wonder Dr. Kennedy had a heart attack!

    I started my work by sharing in the coverage of the general pediatric service. However, my focus was to help get the Pediatric Cardiology unit up and running. Dr. John Collins, who was part of the staff, had made pediatric cardiology his subspecialty interest. He had done some training at The Hospital for Sick Children, Toronto. After returning to St. John's, Dr. Collins resumed his general pediatric practice and supported Dr. Joy in securing a children's hospital in the city. He ranked as a senior physician within the medical staff but had no official title such as 'director' or 'chief' of a clinical service. He had designed and set up a cardiology suite in the basement of the hospital adjacent to radiology. The unit was well planned and included a cardiac catheterization/angiography room, a physician's office, an echocardiography room, and waiting area. Support staff was in place, consisting of a full-time nurse and full-time Echo/EKG Technologist. Dr. Collins had not done any cardiac catheterizations in the new unit, but he quickly organized to do one before I got started. Subsequently, he chose to do very few invasive procedures. Slowly, I got involved in the cardiology clinic schedule, and I became the primary cardiac consultant to the neonatal units across town at Grace Hospital and St. Clare's Hospital, as well as the intensive care unit at the Janeway. This consultation work provided patients that needed an invasive investigation, so I began cardiac catheterization procedures. I should note that echocardiographic imaging was in its infancy at this point and not available to me.

The equipment in the radiology suite gave us problems from the beginning as it was outdated before installation. The angiographic camera had frequent breakdowns, making it difficult to obtain a complete study and adequate information. The support staff was marvelous through all of this. It would be ten years before we acquired two-dimensional echocardiography, an event which revolutionized our approach to cardiac investigation, especially in newborns and infants. The initial ultrasound equipment in the hospital was a Picker 'wobbler' unit, acquired by Radiology, which I was permitted to borrow, if available. Eventually, we were allowed to purchase a unit which was designed specifically for pediatric cardiac work. The only cardiac surgeries done on children before I arrived were a few closed procedures, i.e., procedures that did not require creating an opening in the heart. Any child requiring open heart technique was shipped out to Halifax, Montreal, or Toronto.

By the end of summer, I was comfortably settled into the medical community and also into church life at First Baptist Church. We had intended to take our time on choosing a church by visiting around, but after our visit to First Baptist, we felt so welcome and so at home that we were soon part of the leadership team there. Under the direction of Pastor Morris Russell, the leadership was strong and mature in its approach. The church was blossoming with a vibrant ministry that included challenging evangelical preaching, Sunday school and youth programs, visitation, open air ministry during the summer months, radio and TV ministry, and a daily devotion ministry that the public could avail of via telephone. Later the church became involved in the building of a senior citizen's home, which also proved very successful.

In late August 1967, only two months after I arrived, Dr. Joy advised me, privately, that he was planning to resign as Chief of Staff at the Janeway, on January 1, 1968. He indicated he was planning to write to the medical advisory committee and recommend me as his replacement. Dr. Cliff Joy was an excellent, dedicated pediatrician, and totally committed

35. Dr. C. J. Joy

to making the Janeway Child Health Centre a success. As mentioned earlier, to strengthen his cause he became a member of Premier Joey Smallwood's Government in the Provincial Legislature so he could speak directly on health care matters.

I did not know him well, except by reputation, and had only met him in the spring of 1965, as I was preparing to leave Newfoundland for my training in Oregon. I attended a social gathering at his home and got to know his family a bit better. They must have come to trust me because, a year later, they called me for help with a family problem. Nobody was available to pick up their teenage son from summer camp in Ontario. Mrs. Joy phoned and asked if I was free on the weekend to fly to Toronto to meet the boy, and told me the arrangements she had made. I flew to Toronto and met him at the Royal York Hotel. We stayed overnight and next morning caught a plane back to Newfoundland. The plane stopped in Montreal, and I took advantage of the stop and left the plane to call Betty's parents. I must have misunderstood the departure time because when I returned to board the plane the gate was closed, and I could see the aircraft, with the boy on board, moving away. I was mortified and desperate as I negotiated with the airline attendant to get me on the next flight to St. John's. I did get back about two hours after the boy was safely home and you can imagine my embarrassment at having to explain things to the Joy family. They were good sports, and we all laughed at my faux pas.

Once the rumor got out regarding Dr. Joy's plans to resign, the political rumblings started, and I knew that some of the pediatricians, all of whom were senior to me, were unhappy with his recommendation that I, a junior greenhorn, should replace him. One of them was even so bold as to come to my office and privately tell me I should not agree to the proposal. Dr. Joy was resolute in his decision and had a fearless devotion to seeing the hospital succeed. I objected, but he indicated, regardless he would send forward his recommendation, which he did.

The Medical Advisory Committee (MAC) was composed of chiefs of the various clinical services. As I remember them, they included Dr. Walter Heneghan (Radiology), Dr. Richard Kennedy (Surgery), Dr. Charles Henderson (Anesthesia), Dr. Charles Boddie (Psychiatry), Dr. John Collins (Cardiology), Dr. Charles Hutton (Laboratory Services), Dr. Joy, and Mr. Kelland (Administrator). While I felt reasonably regarded by most of the MAC members, I knew that Dr. Joy's proposal would not go unchallenged.

While the above was brewing at the hospital, another momentous medical announcement occurred for Newfoundland. In 1961, the Federal Government of Canada received a report of a Royal Commission on Health, headed by Justice Hall, which recommended that they establish a second medical school in the Atlantic region. In the six years following this report the Canadian Government received recommendations regarding the location of the new school and the choice had been narrowed down to New Brunswick (Moncton) or Newfoundland (St. John's). In 1966, Lord Brain was appointed by the Newfoundland Government as a Royal Commission to review the Hall Commission recommendations, and he confirmed that a medical school was 'crucial for Newfoundland.' Dr. Ian Rusted (1921-2007), a prominent Internist in St. John's, had spearheaded the case for his Province.

On September 1st, 1967, the announcement was made that Memorial University (St. John's) had won, and Dr. Rusted would become the Dean of the new school. This news changed the political environment for the medical community in St. John's. It meant that the new Professor and Chairman of Pediatrics at Memorial would become the Physician in Chief at the Janeway hospital. Before Christmas 1967, Dr. John Darte from Toronto was identified as the leading candidate for this position. As a result, I was appointed as Interim Chief of Medicine (Pediatrics) to succeed Dr. Joy on January 1, 1968. A month later Dr. Darte accepted the University appointment, and he asked me to continue in an interim role at the hospital until he could relocate to St. John's in September. I did my best to fulfill this significant role and was in constant communication with him as I dealt with administrative issues. There were immediate pressures from staff members wanting recognition as directors of various subspecialty interests, in the belief that such recognition would strengthen their consideration for academic appointment at the new medical school. I met with several who wanted such recognition. It was difficult because of their seniority to me regarding age, years of practice, and service to the people of the Island. I could only reassure them they would be dealt with fairly but, in truth, such appointments had to wait until September. For myself, I had no assurances regarding my status once Dr. Darte arrived. Through the spring and summer, I followed a 'steady as she goes' administrative plan. I was now a member of the Medical Advisory Committee and witness to many decision delays pending the arrival of Dr. Darte.

Cliff Joy remained a close support to me in the months after he announced his plan to resign as Chief of Staff, and his support continued throughout my career in St. John's. He relocated to Niagara Falls for a time but then returned and resumed practice in the city where he specialized in allergy. But, the stress of getting the Janeway started, plus the pressures of his time in politics, took its toll on his health which deteriorated significantly in subsequent years and led to his untimely death in 1994.

CHAPTER 24

Our Life In St. John's

(1967 - 1977)

DURING THE MONTHS LEADING UP to September 1968, my life was busy. We were exploring the housing market for a home so we could move out of the Janeway Apartments. In November 1967, we found a bungalow close to the hospital, and I applied to my chosen bank for a mortgage, but they denied funding. My committed income from the Janeway was only seventy-five hundred dollars for the first year, plus whatever fee-for-service income I could generate. At that point the latter was small (I'd been in town only three months) so my bank was nervous. I consulted a pediatric colleague, and he contacted his bank manager who gladly approved my application. We secured the bungalow at 8 Derby Place for $28,000, and this became our first permanent home. While Betty was busy looking after our two small children (Gregory and Caroline) and getting the house decorated, I was getting more active at the hospital with administrative responsibilities and building up my clinical practice. Betty and I were now very involved in the life of First Baptist Church and began overseeing the Young People's program. Every Friday night we chaperoned the senior young people and drove them home after their meeting. In the New Year, I was elected to the Board of the Church, and this continued for the next several years. Betty enjoyed activities with the women and choir. Sunday became as busy as Monday so that the only free time I had to do things around the home was Saturday afternoon. Before long I was also involved in the Newfoundland Medical Association (NMA) as an executive member and took on the responsibility of Honorary Secretary, a position I held for several years. One year I was asked to become President of the NMA but declined because I was overcommitted and not spending enough time with my family. The Heart and Stroke Foundation nominated me to represent the Province at the National level, and I became a member of their Grants Panel. This panel reviewed research grant applications each year before and during committee meetings, usually in Ottawa, where awards were approved. One year I tried to travel to Ottawa for a meeting in February but was stuck in Halifax for over twenty-four hours due to an ice storm, and the meeting was just finishing when I arrived in Ottawa.

When Dr. John Darte got settled in September 1968, I was relieved to be free of administrative responsibilities at the hospital. I could now focus on strengthening the pediatric cardiology service and preparing for whatever teaching responsibilities were assigned to me when the new medical school started classes. Dr. Darte was a giant, not just physically, but professionally and as a human being. When we walked the corridors of the hospital together, it was truly a 'Mutt and Jeff' situation. He was a world authority in blood disorders (hematology) and the management of childhood cancer. I tried to brief him fully on the unresolved staffing issues. I moved from the big office down a couple of doors and continued to meet with him and share what I knew about each staff member and the political environment of the hospital.

36. Dr. J. M. Darte

His arrival meant a considerable change in my income. The hospital, in elevating me to Acting Chief of Medicine required me to turn back any fee-for-service revenue but increased my stipend to sixty thousand dollars a year; something that was a 'princely sum' in Newfoundland considering I had no office overhead. Following Dr. Darte's arrival, the hospital extended my salaried arrangement until he decided on my university status. His decision came just before Christmas 1968 when he offered me a full-time appointment as Assistant Professor of Pediatrics and an annual salary of twenty-three thousand and five hundred dollars, plus the use of a free office in the hospital and secretarial support as needed. Naturally, this represented a significant adjustment, but I was allowed to retain my fee-for-service income again, and this cushioned the differential somewhat.

The University made plans to admit the first class of medical students in September 1970. Late in 1968, Dr. Darte and I began what we thought would be a relaxed two-year planning of curriculum for the new school. However, the Minister of Health was openly questioning the financial viability of the project and threatening to close it down. Dr. Rusted, as Dean, decided to attempt an end run by admitting the first students one year earlier than planned, i.e. in September 1969, reasoning that if a class of students got selected it would be political suicide for the Government to stop it. To accomplish this, we had to open the admissions process immediately to screen and accept students for the first class. At the same time, we had to fast-track curriculum planning. In Pediatrics, we hardly kept ahead of the process and found ourselves planning what we would teach, and by whom, within hours of the student's admission. For the rest of the first academic year, we struggled to keep pace with the teaching needs. The first class consisted of twenty-three bright students who were a joy to work with and some became prominent leaders in the profession after graduation.

Dr. Darte also set about identifying roles and the academic status of each member of the Pediatric staff and recruited additions to strengthen some subspecialty needs. All of the established Pediatricians were given Senior or Clinical (non-salaried) appointments to faculty. Other sections of the staff (e.g. Laboratory Medicine and Pathology, Radiology, Surgery, Orthopedics, and Psychiatry), were given appointment to the appropriate faculty department as organized at the university level. The Janeway was the first hospital in the city to sign an Academic teaching agreement with the University. I was asked to serve on several university committees dealing with curriculum planning and designing and integrating the schedule of instruction for each year.

On a personal note, I found Dr. Darte to be a fantastic chairperson. He was kind, considerate and friendly to all of us and regularly joined us for a coffee break in the cafeteria at 10:30 each morning when, for about half an hour or so, physicians from throughout the hospital attempted to gather, connect, and discuss the internal and external news of the day.

St. John's had an active 'Irish element' within its physician population, i.e., persons who were of Irish descent and had trained in the medical school at Dublin, and the Janeway had its fair share of members from this group. Individually, they had a great sense of humor combined with a skeptical, even cynical, attitude to whatever or whoever was popular 'fodder'. They were untrusting of colleagues, hospital administration, government, the university, and especially the new medical Dean. Every idea or proposal from any source was immediately suspect. In true Newfoundland fashion at the time, based on years of political betrayal, it was accepted that every new plan had an ulterior motive which had to be discovered by 'looking under the carpet' to identify what it might be. Rumors were generated to fuel the intensity of discussion so that, in just a few days, every seemingly good or progressive idea was wrapped in layers of suspected dirt. Dr. Darte loved to join in these 'bull sessions' and I'm sure they provided great insight to him on the temperament of the medical staff. Of course, he was the object of suspicion himself; a 'come from away' person parachuted into this boiler pot environment. Nevertheless, I can truthfully say that, from the beginning, his stellar personality and love for the Janeway shone through, and his motives were never suspect. Some of the other Professors and Chairmen, who were brought in from elsewhere, were not so fortunate or highly regarded. There was a cynical labeling of them as 'Air Canada Professors', a reference to their frequent absences from St. John's 'with return just long enough to pick up their mail'. I am not sure how they regarded me but felt they were puzzled that I had given up 'power' so quietly and was concentrating on patient care rather than medical politics.

Dr. Darte and his wife, Margaret, bought a home on Rennie's Mill Road in the old town area close to Government House. They were wonderful hosts and held numerous social functions to foster friendship within Pediatrics. Margaret threw herself into the life of the hospital. She was instrumental in establishing a Hospital Auxiliary, and organizing 'Janeway Day at the Races' – a function which continued for several years and formed the basis for a fundraising campaign that became a Charitable Foundation for the hospital; which continues to this day.

Dr. Darte had a struggle with controlling his weight and with smoking. He had played football as a lineman at college and now had some difficulty with both his knees and hips as a result. It was amusing, but sad, to be with him during the times he attempted to diet and quit smoking simultaneously. He would come into the office, sit at his desk and start strumming his fingers in animated fashion in a desperate attempt to find something to do with his hands. He would be thinking through some problem and scratch the back of his head and neck to keep occupied. You could sense the tension he was controlling in his tendency to become irritable, a feature that was not normally him. I would see him get up and pace down the hall through the nearby wards just for something to do. Invariably his attempt to end smoking failed and his attempt at dieting got negated by having to attend receptions and 'rubber chicken' dinners as part of his job. Sometimes I would wander into his office when he was in such a state, and he would grin back at me as he struggled and confessed what was going on in his life at that point. I tried to be a vent source and solace to him without ever invading his privacy or betraying his confidence.

In 1975, Dr. Darte accepted an appointment at the Princess Margaret Hospital in Toronto and returned there as an executive in the cancer field. I never saw him after he left St. John's but I did have contact with his wife, Margaret, a few years later after he died. Some time later I painted a picture of him which I felt was of reasonable quality, so I offered it to the hospital.

I was pleased when the hospital administrator wrote on behalf of the Board to advise they had gladly accepted the painting, and later it greeted attendees at the entrance to a new conference room. Several years later, after moving to Hamilton, I was invited back to work at the hospital for a couple of weeks, while the regular cardiologist was away, and was asked to participate in grand rounds in the new conference room. My painting greeted me in the entrance hall. Later again, when the Janeway moved to its present Health Sciences location, my painting was transferred to the provincial archives building called 'The Rooms' in downtown St. John's as part of the early records of the Janeway. Efforts are now being made to have the painting returned to the new Children's Hospital and hung in an appropriate place, and I hope that this will happen as a tribute to the medical school's founding Professor of Pediatrics, who was a great human being.

During my short time as acting Chairman of Pediatrics, the hospital administrator asked me to write a document entitled *The Future of the Janeway* in which I recommended that the Children's Hospital become an integral part of the Health Sciences Complex scheduled for building on the campus of Memorial University. My document was considered by the board of the hospital and was implemented later after I moved away.

The departure of Dr. Darte changed the Janeway environment considerably. He had done an excellent job of uniting us as a team as we had confidence in his leadership and motivation. After he had left, I was again appointed as acting chief of Pediatrics at the hospital, and Bert Davis became acting Chairman of the University Department. Bert had a flair for administration while my skills were clinical care. I already had enough on my plate and did not bother to apply for 'higher office'. The arrangement worked well for the duration that we needed to find a new Professor and Chairman. Besides, I was due for a sabbatical leave and wanted to be free to take advantage of the opportunity to refresh my skills and knowledge in pediatric cardiology. I was on friendly terms with the senior cardiologists at The Hospital for Sick Children, Toronto, especially Dr. Richard Rowe and Dr. Robert Freedom, so a plan was made to do a Fellowship there from July

1977 - June 1978 as the professional component of my sabbatical year. We now had four children, two of whom were on the brink of adolescence, and this was a significant consideration as we planned for our leave. Gregory was twelve and completing grade seven. Caroline was nearly eleven and about to complete grade six. Susan was eight and doing grade three but struggling and in need of some individual tutoring, while Steven was just two and developing normally.

In the meantime in 1976, Dr. Donald Hillman was identified as the new Professor and Chairman of Pediatrics. On arrival, it was clear that he was operating at the university level, as distinct from the hospital level, and his principal advisor on local affairs was Bert Davis, with me having a minor role at the hospital. His wife, Dr. Elizabeth (Liz) Hillman, also a pediatrician, came as part of the package. They were inseparable in both visibility and action. Their joint involvement in decision making introduced some irritation within the hospital community. I knew Don and Liz from my training days at The Montreal Children's Hospital. They were part of the staff there where Don was a consultant in endocrine disorders while Liz was in charge of the outpatient clinics. I worked with Liz during my year as Chief Resident, and also during the subsequent year when I worked as a Fellow in cardiology clinics. Our relationship in Montreal was cordial but reserved. I had no problem with Don, but he was not the fuzzy bear I was accustomed to with Dr. Darte and did not command the same level of respect. He was small and short, a bit dwarfish in appearance, and came across as somewhat indecisive. Behind his back, he was referred to as 'little Donnie'. During ward rounds one day, he and a group of students were standing at the bed of a small boy and discussing the boy's problem. The boy suddenly pipes up and says, 'Are you little Donnie?' There were embarrassed snickers in the group.

Liz was a friendly outgoing person who wanted to please and help in every situation. Unfortunately, her enthusiastic approach generated a degree of irritation in many of the staff, including me. Many people viewed her desire to contribute as pre-emptive and meddling in situations involving both administration and clinical care. Don did not appear free of her mothering presence and influence in his administrative role. Myself, I found it difficult to deal privately with him as Liz had the knack, at the critical moment, of opening the closed door and becoming involved in the discussion and influencing the decision-making.

I was glad, therefore, that the Faculty administration had granted me permission for a sabbatical leave before Don's arrival. The hospital had recruited Dr. Shyama Virmani as a second Pediatric Cardiologist, so coverage for my absence was in place. Dr. John Collins was still part of the staff but mostly confined himself to an office practice uptown and rarely did any clinical work in cardiology at the hospital.

I had hoped that we could develop a limited program in Cardiac Surgery for children at the Janeway. When I arrived in St. John's no open heart surgery had occurred on children. A few surgeons with pediatric training and skills had performed some closed procedures. When the new medical school recruited a cardiac surgeon as Professor and Chairman of Surgery, and his wife was advertised as a cardiac surgeon with specialized skills in pediatric work. Their appointment was announced in March 1968 with effect in September, coinciding with the arrival of Dr. Darte. I was excited and felt this meant we would be able to repair a variety of less complex cardiac defects at the Janeway. I started to collect a list of patients for surgery in anticipation of moving forward in this area. By joint agreement between the hospitals, the General Hospital bought a pump-oxygenator that could serve the needs of adults and children and hired an experienced technician to run the equipment. We worked with the blood bank to secure adequate reserves for the pediatric patients, and everything appeared underway towards start up. The operating room nurses, anesthetists, and intensive care staff were all trained and ready for participation. But, there was a problem. Looking back on it now, it appears we had hired reluctant surgeons. I never discovered the basis for this reluctance but every time a child was scheduled, even admitted to hospital and prepared, they seemed to find a reason to cancel and defer surgery indefinitely. The delaying went on for at least two years so that all levels of staff became discouraged and suspicious. Fortunately, none of the patients were critically ill or died as a result of the delay, and we transferred to Halifax any patients who needed or requested such action. This surgical team stayed for five years, until 1973, and then returned to the United States. During that time, only a few cardiac surgical procedures were done on children. It was not until Dr. Gary Cornell came from Ottawa that we were able to get the program under way, and he did a marvelous job in this area. Gary was a very careful and caring surgeon who was prepared to sit at the bedside of his patients in recovery and intensive care for twenty-four hours, if necessary, to monitor and ensure that they received proper management. He worked closely with Shyama Virmani, who also came from Ottawa, and they were excellent as a team.

In the spring of 1977, things were finally in place for my sabbatical year at Sick Kids, Toronto. Dr. Virmani had not found a house and was living in rented quarters, so she agreed to look after our home and live there during our absence. Our sabbatical year also meant we would get a breather from our busy church life in St. John's. Betty and I were chaperoning the senior young people, and I was still in leadership on the Board of Deacons. Also, in 1973, the church had obtained a mortgage to build a senior citizens facility, and I was part of the management board for this new home. The project proceeded well, on time and budget; something that represented a miracle in Newfoundland. Then, in 1975, as the home neared completion, Pastor Russell accepted a call to a church in Toronto. His departure meant added responsibilities for the deacons. I was asked to chair the search committee to find a new pastor and, for the next year, we conducted a seemingly fruitless search. Then in late summer, 1976, a couple of our deacons were vacationing in Maine and encountered a young street preacher that attracted their interest. They talked with him, found out about his background and training, and rushed home to persuade the search committee that he be invited to preach for a call as pastor.

He came. He preached. But, the Search Committee could not agree to endorse him for a call. A church meeting was convened to advise the congregation, and after a lively discussion, a motion was introduced to extend a call to him, contrary to the Search Committee's inability to so recommend. A vote occurred and carried by one vote over the 2/3 majority required. As chairperson, I was asked to inform the candidate of the result, and he accepted to come as pastor in September 1976. I should note that this was an unusual acceptance as most pastoral candidates would decline appointment with anything less than an eighty-five-percent support vote.

The new pastor was a good personal evangelist but, administratively and overall, proved a disaster for the church. In the next nine months, before I left for my sabbatical, he alienated some of the leadership and core members. He tampered with the church's affiliation and constitution. He meddled with the administration of the new senior's home (Escasoni) and was unhappy that the church was involved in operating such a project. The leadership culture that he had trained under, and brought to the church, was dictatorial in style and foreign to our environment. All of my leadership responsibilities ended before departing for Toronto.

CHAPTER 25

Our Sabbatical Year In Toronto

(JULY 1977 - JUNE 1978)

In June 1977, we packed our van with essential belongings, including winter clothing, and the six of us headed for the ferry in Argentia and the drive to Montreal. After our customary stopover with Betty's parents, we arrived in Toronto and began searching for an apartment. I had hoped to find a place close to the Hospital for Sick Children ('SickKids'), but schools for the children were an issue. Eventually, we found living space in a high-rise apartment at Islington and the 401 expressway. This location meant an hour commute to the Hospital by bus and subway each morning. It made for a long day, especially when rounds began at 7:00 AM and, in the evening, I got home after 7:00 PM because of rush hour and other factors. It was tough being a trainee again. The expectations of our supervisors were high. Dr. Richard Rowe, the chief, was a real gentleman and master clinician, and I never had any worries about him. Dr. Robert Freedom, the second in command, was a good friend but, as a professional supervisor, he expected the best out of everybody. In the Catheterization Lab, where he was the supervisor and monitored the quality of investigations, he did not hesitate to require additional work if he felt something was unclear. I took my turn at doing procedures every fourth month. Fortunately, I was experienced and reasonably skilled at catheter insertions in blood vessels. We usually investigated two or three patients each weekday, depending on complexity. A report had to be prepared after each investigation and readied for presentation next morning at a staff conference. Any patients needing surgery had to be presented again at another gathering with the surgeons. Conference presentations were a tense time as your work might get criticized and sent back for supplementary studies if the surgical team was not happy with the data. I acquitted myself well during the year and was able to return to St. John's better informed and skilled in dealing with the more complex cases.

For my family, the year was an adventure. We lived on the 7th floor of a large high-rise apartment in the northwest section of the city and about an hour from the hospital. We arrived with practically no furniture but quickly acquired second-hand bedding, basic kitchen utensils and dishes. Gradually we added a second-hand TV and other items as needed. We had an enjoyable experience with the church during the year. Thistletown Baptist Church warmly received us. A couple of families were from Newfoundland and that made us feel at home. The church was very hospitable and helped us find second-hand things as needed.

Selecting schools for the children was a bit of a problem. The environment in nearby schools varied considerably. Our two oldest children (Gregory and Caroline) were close to completing High School in Newfoundland but in Ontario, there were thirteen grades, instead of eleven, so their placements were in grades where they had already done much of the work. Their assignments made for a rather dull experience, resulting in a loss of motivation. On returning to St. John's they were 'out of sync' with the classmates they had left, and were not permitted in the advanced level classes they had left. Thus, for them, the year significantly gummed up their high school education. Susan received the attention she needed during the year and did well, with no ill effects from the change. Steven had not yet started school.

I recall a couple of incidents. One day as we drove along Eglington Avenue, near our apartment, a police car suddenly appeared behind me, put on his flashers, and pulled me over. I had not been speeding so the surprise made me very nervous. I could not think of what I had done wrong. The two officers in the car approached from behind, one on the driver's side and the other on the passenger side. Betty was with me, and she rolled down the passenger window to be greeted by a grinning officer who whispered to her not to be alarmed. Meanwhile, the officer on my side asked for my license, which I produced. He asked me where my home was in Newfoundland. I told him, and he too smiled and said he just wanted to meet a fellow 'Newfie.' He had spotted my Newfoundland license plates.

The second incident happened in the apartment. The children had bought a pet hamster. One day 'Joey' went missing and we thought he had fallen from the balcony to the ground seven floors below. Betty and the children inspected the gallery and, looking down, saw several blobs on the grass that they thought might be Joey. The children were sent to investigate, but the blobs were not the hamster. A couple of days went by and Betty was again on the balcony. Suddenly Joey appeared, safe and sound, out of a hole in a bag of dirt she had bought for some plants. All was well, and we had a good laugh.

My year in Toronto was very tiring because of the daily commute plus the long hours at the hospital. When spring arrived, I began to look forward to our return to St. John's. The year had been profitable for me but, unfortunately, it was a lost year for our older children as regards their schooling. Betty had enjoyed the change of environment but living in a seventh-floor apartment with four children was not always comfortable. So, as June 1978 approached, we were excited about packing up and heading east. During the trip, we visited with Betty's parents in Montreal and then stopped at Lake Wallace to visit friends from Sherbrooke before going to Nova Scotia and the ferry back home. It was wonderful to set foot on the rock, as Newfoundland is called, and renew friendships with relatives and associates in St. John's. I was looking forward to traveling again to do clinics across the island and 'down north' - the local expression for going to St. Anthony and Labrador.

Throughout the year, we were in touch with friends in St. John's who updated us about ongoing events at First Baptist Church. The young minister was attracting a lot of attention with his preaching style, and the congregation was growing. At Christmas, the church received extra attention by creating an outdoor nativity scene which included live animals – some of which got loose for a time - but at Easter, 1978, the pastor created a crisis. He refused permission for a priest to say mass at Escasoni, where about 80% of the residents were Catholic. Next day the provincial government seized ownership of the home, citing 'religious discrimination' by the staff. The adverse publicity generated by this event destroyed the good reputation and name of Baptists in Newfoundland. At this writing, nearly forty years later, the Baptist churches in the province are still struggling to recover.

CHAPTER 26

The Last Years In St. John's

(July 1978 – March 1981)

～⌘～

ON OUR RETURN FROM TORONTO, we found our home in good shape. Dr. Virmani had not lived there the full year, but she left it in good order and friends did regular inspections for us. Betty and the children settled back into home life in St. John's. However, for all of us, things had changed significantly.

Firstly, our church life underwent a dramatic change. Emotionally, it was very traumatic not to feel welcome back at the church which had been our home for the previous ten years. We loved First Baptist Church, and still do, but we felt led to move to West End Baptist, a welcoming church with a slightly different flavor. The people were very kind and friendly, and Betty and I were invited to serve in ministry. It met our needs well for the balance of our time in St. John's.

For the children, especially our two oldest, the return to school was a disappointment. They had been in advanced classes previously, but now were placed in standard classes and the curriculum was not as challenging. This downgrade at school resulted in a loss of motivation, as had developed in Toronto so that their final years of schooling were affected.

I found my work conditions at the Janeway, and the University were also different. At the hospital, Don and Liz were in charge, and Bert Davis was Don's primary local advisor. So I no longer had any administrative role in either the hospital or faculty. My work in cardiology was lighter as Dr. Virmani had proven to be an excellent addition and we shared equally in clinical responsibilities. At the university, I enjoyed the resumption of teaching activity with lectures and tutorials for the medical students. I still had some involvement in the Newfoundland Medical Association and The Heart and Stroke Foundation but not as deeply as previously. We enjoyed our clinical and diagnostic work in Cardiology but had to curtail the plans for children's heart surgery until Dr. Gary Cornell arrived towards the end of my time.

In the fall of 1978, I traveled to Vancouver and attended the meetings of the Canadian Cardiovascular Society. While there I met Dr. Arnold Johnson, who had been one of my mentors at The Montreal Children's Hospital. He was now Chief of Cardiology at McMaster University. During a conversation, he informed me they were interested in recruiting a pediatric cardiologist to their staff. Would I be interested? My reply was that anything he was involved with was always of interest to me. He was a pioneer in pediatric cardiology, having trained at John's Hopkins University with Drs.Taussig and Blalock who were pioneers in the diagnosis and surgical treatment of children with congenital heart disease. He was like a father figure to me, and I always felt comfortable with him.

I went back to St. John's and did not think much about our conversation. About a month later, the phone rang one evening, and it was Dr. Alvin Zipursky, Professor of Pediatrics at McMaster. Dr. Johnson had spoken to him, and he wanted me to come to Hamilton and see if I might be a good fit for their plans for pediatric cardiology. I discussed the proposal with Betty, and we decided this was worth further exploration.

It was ironic that ten years earlier, in 1967, while completing my training in Oregon I had contacted the Physician in Chief at The Hamilton General Hospital, to see if there would be an interest in me. The Chief indicated a potential interest but only after I obtained recognition as a specialist in pediatrics, i.e. had become a Fellow of the Royal College of Physicians of Canada. I was a 'certified' specialist but had not yet attained the status of 'fellow.' At that time, there was a two-tiered Royal College qualification for consultants - certification vs. fellowship; those with certificates were suitable for practice but those granted Fellowship were suitable for academic positions as well as practice. This policy was generating some controversy, and The Canadian Medical Association Journal (CMAJ) was drawing attention to the issue. It published a letter to the editor titled *The Brain Drip* (October 1, 1966, Vol. 95, page 734) indicating the policy resulted in many excellent young Canadian consultants choosing to remain in the USA rather than return home. More letters appeared in subsequent weeks, and I made a contribution (CMAJ, Jan 7, 1967, Vol. 96, page 55) which may have enhanced my being unsuitable for academic appointment. The controversy smoldered for a while, and a few years later the Royal College made it possible to buy one's Fellowship following certification. At the time, I did not appreciate that the Chief of Medicine did not represent the Faculty of Health Sciences at McMaster, but a letter from Dr. John Evans, Dean, set me straight when he chastised me for accusing him of a restrictive hiring policy for faculty.

Our exploration of a move to Hamilton involved several visits over the next eighteen months. During my first visit to McMaster, I met Dr. Zipursky and senior members of the Faculty of Health Sciences, several pediatricians, and cardiologists. I did not rush into accepting an appointment but tried to assess all options and consequences of any move. Emotionally, I was firmly committed to remaining in Newfoundland despite the stagnant nature of things professionally and the discouragement from the problems at church.

For the next two years, I remained unsettled in my situation in St. John's. Professionally, the prospects for improvement in cardiology services at the hospital were non-existent due to financial constraints and low priority, as judged by the hospital administration. We had settled well into the congregation at West End Baptist Church, and felt useful there, but it was not the same as being in the company of our long-time friends at First Baptist. As much as I was a Newfoundlander at heart and wanted to stay in St. John's, when 1980 arrived, I felt that a change would be better for me, and Betty felt the same. I wrestled with the decision for nearly another year. My relations with Don and Liz never improved and, in all honesty, I was not confident in their leadership at the Janeway, and this did not foster the motivation I had to do my best for its future.

On November 1st, 1980, I wrote my letter of resignation and advised Don I wished to leave effective December 31st.

As soon as he heard the news, Dean Rusted wrote me a personal note expressing his great regret at my decision. His letter indicated he understood some of the things that were troubling me. I advised McMaster of my decision to accept appointment there and Dr. Zipursky set in motion the steps needed to welcome me in January. Dr. Hillman, for his part, advised me that he could not release me on January 1st and wanted me to stay until mid-march. I never received any reasons for this, but I accepted his decision and began preparing for our move to Hamilton.

CHAPTER 27

Our Years At McMaster University

(1981 - 1999)

––&––

IN NOVEMBER 1980, WE BEGAN the process of preparing to leave St. John's. First, there was the sale of our home. Finding a buyer was going to be a difficult problem because mortgage interest rates at the time hovered between eighteen and twenty-two percent. Our house was big but not modern in the sense of being recently built. It began life as a large bungalow with a finished basement, but it was given a second story with a peaked roof a few years before I bought it. The upstairs contained large drafty windows which whistled and creaked in the wind and were a source of high heat loss. The roof insulation was incomplete in some areas, and while I had done my best to improve it, there was a need for a professional touch. I began searching for a house in Hamilton and discovered we would have to pay more than we could expect from our home in St. John's. Also, if I did not sell, I would end up with bridge financing and pay two mortgages with high interest for an indefinite period.

The education of our children, especially our two oldest (Gregory and Caroline), who were in the middle of grades eleven and ten respectively, was an additional concern. A move to Ontario meant extending their high school time to grade thirteen, something they were not happy to contemplate. We were not as concerned about the placements for our two younger children even though Susan needed some support with understanding concepts in a few areas. Our youngest, Steven, was just beginning school and had no learning issues.

My colleagues and friends were very kind as we went through the process of leaving. The people at West End Baptist Church were exceptionally helpful as we completed the two years with them and favored us with a reception.

By Christmas Day, 1980, we had packed our belongings, and a moving van had come and taken our furniture, bedding and summer clothing, and started down the road to Hamilton. On Boxing Day, the six of us started the drive across Newfoundland to the ferry at Port aux Basque and then to Montreal. The trip went smoothly, and we encountered clear roads and good weather. We left our dog, Joey, in a kennel in St. John's. When we reached Montreal, we took a couple of days to visit with Betty's parents. On New Year's Day, 1981, we drove to Hamilton and, as our furniture did not arrive on schedule, took rooms in the old Connaught Hotel. Next day we secured the keys to our new home in Ancaster, near Hamilton, and took possession. After a day or so I had to leave Betty with the task of awaiting our furniture, getting settled into the new home and sorting out the placement of the children in schools. Fortunately, as she accompanied Steven to school, our new backyard neighbor befriended her and provided blankets and utensils to use until our furniture arrived. The family slept on the floor for a couple of nights.

I flew back to St. John's and spent the next ten weeks in our empty house with Joey. We were both lonely and good company for each other. I slept on the floor with the dog beside me. I was now into the dreaded situation of having no potential buyers interested in our home, so I was carrying two mortgages and bridge financing. I put in my time at the hospital, but January is always a slow month after the holiday break. My colleagues, like me, could not figure out why I had been held back from leaving with my family, but I kept quiet through it all. Dr. Virmani was handling the

Cardiology load. After serving out the requested time until mid-March, I was finally able to pack our other car and, with Joey, start the long drive back to Hamilton. Most of the Pediatricians met and held a farewell reception for me and presented me with several gifts.

The second winter trip to Ontario was more treacherous than the first. The road across Newfoundland was clear, but the car did not have winter tires. Consequently, whenever I felt I was traveling on ice, or the wind was high, I would cut my speed to avoid skidding. The road approaching Port Aux Basque can be very dangerous in winter because of cross winds and black ice. I encountered some of this and had to be careful not to get blown into oncoming traffic or skid off the road. The ferry crossing to Sydney was cold and windy, so I took a cabin and slept for part of the way. Joey had to spend a frigid night in a cage on the rear end of the boat, and I felt real sorry for him. He was very glad to see me in the morning.

The road in Nova Scotia was fairly good until I reached Antigonish. I was in need of gas so, as I was leaving the town, I pulled into a station and filled the tank. I got back on the road and had gone about two kilometers when the unexpected happened. There was little traffic, but a troublesome collection of slush on the center line made steering difficult. As I approached an oncoming car, my front tire got caught in the slush and kept pulling me further into the middle of the road and into the path of the approaching car. I was probably going around eighty kilometers an hour and, in desperation, I yanked the wheel hard right. The tires caught the bare pavement and immediately propelled me into the little snow bank lining the right side of the road. Fortunately, there were no telephone poles or guard rails in the area, so I skidded over the ledge into the gulley and some low brush. A river ran parallel to the road at this point, and a collection of bushes nudged the car's rear leftward and I headed into the river. I went over the embankment and landed in the water. Fortunately, the car didn't roll over, and the river was only about a foot deep at that point. My whole life flashed before me as I realized all that could have happened. Joey did not panic and remained placid through it all. I slowly opened the car door and discovered the water was not over the door sill. I was close to the bank so managed to get out with getting only my feet wet. I headed back to the road to signal the next car that came for help and, as I did, a police car drove up and stopped. A Mountie climbed out and asked if I was hurt. I said no but worried the bottom of my car was damaged even though the motor, which I left running, was sounding normal and there was no sign of gas leaking or loss of oil. She asked for the usual identification and when she saw I was from Newfoundland she smiled and indicated she was also from there. She called a tow truck, and it arrived within ten minutes. The driver inspected the situation and winched the car up to the road without any damage. Joey sat placidly in the front seat observing it all.

After checking the undercarriage, and under the hood, the service man said everything looked good and cleared me to continue on my way. I took a hotel in Moncton for the night where I knew pets were allowed. Joey was calm as we were at ground level and I had a patio door allowing him to go outside as needed. Next day I arrived in Montreal and rested overnight with Betty's parents. It was no problem to complete the trip to Hamilton, and it felt good to be together again with my family. The children were excited to have Joey back, and he expressed mutual feelings to them.

I was greeted with a surprise when I arrived at McMaster. For several months, I had been negotiating with Dr. Alvin Zipursky as Chairman of Pediatrics. He was an excellent individual who skillfully arranged my contract identical to what I was leaving at Memorial University. The negotiation was somewhat tricky as regards to rank because McMaster did not

37. My car in the river. March 1981, near Antigonish, NS.

appoint new people to the rank of Professor unless they were coming in as chairperson of a discipline or department. Pediatric Cardiology did not have recognition as such at the time. But, unknown to me, Dr. Zipursky had resigned to accept an appointment at SickKids only a month before I was due to arrive. When I contacted McMaster to let them know about my delayed arrival, I discovered the new Chief of Pediatrics was Dr. Peter Dent. Naturally, I had some apprehensions but found him a most gracious gentleman who, without question, honored the agreements I had reached with his predecessor. Peter and his wife, Dianne, did everything possible to make our transition to Hamilton a good experience. He was most understanding about my delayed arrival, and Dianne did her best to help Betty get settled and feel at home. It was somewhat like working with Dr. Darte again. I was given a bright office next door to Dr. Bill Wilson, another gentleman, and we shared a very excellent secretary. Initially, I had to share investigative services with adult cardiology, but this was not a handicap as there were technologists trained to deal with children. Clinic space was just across the hall from my office, and nursing support was good.

38. McMaster ID photo, March 1981

Work at McMaster was like a holiday compared to my schedule at the Janeway. I now had Saturday and Sunday 'free' even though I was on call seven days a week. The staff respected my weekends and called me only if they were desperate for help with a newborn. Fortunately, echocardiography had improved so the investigation of children was relatively easy and I could provide reliable information to the caregivers without having to spend hours with the patient.

Most of my educational responsibilities occurred in Jan-Feb-March of each year. In those months, I tutored 6-8 students twice a week while they solved clinical problems through self-directed research and group discussion. My primary role was to keep the students on track and steer the conversation in the right direction so they could maximize the use of time and end up with a satisfactory knowledge base and management skills. Other educational activities involved supervising residents and learners in the clinic, and lecturing groups about congenital heart disease at a post graduate level. Research activity was challenging, but I was able to collaborate with the Neonatal team who had cardiology related projects in progress

There was a problem with cardiac catheterization services. The facilities were located several kilometers away at the Hamilton General Hospital (HGH) and were excellent but designed for adult procedures. The hospital required that all cardiac catheterizations procedures have support from anesthesia, at least on a stand-by basis. I had rarely needed this for pediatric procedures, using a sedative cocktail instead, as was the practice in most Children's Hospitals in North America. Scheduling backup from anesthesia was a problem because only some of the staff anesthetists were comfortable with handling children and this, together with the hassle of having to transport patients by ambulance across town, and back again, had the effect of shutting down my catheterization work after only a couple of attempts. Also, I quickly realized that such procedures would be repeated at SickKids if a child needed surgery, so I was putting myself, and the patient, through unnecessary stress by attempting to do this work.

I encountered a similar problem concerning sedation of small children for echocardiograms. Again, in most Children's Hospitals, it was common to use chloral hydrate as short-term sedation for such investigation. We recognized, and warned parents, that sometimes this sedative had the opposite effect of sending the children into a rage state so that they would not settle for the procedure. The Nursing Department studied the problem and decided that Chloral Hydrate was unsafe for use as a primary sedative. Their decision caused a temporary stoppage in sedated procedures until they trained a team and set up a special unit to administer sedation. The ironic thing was, and is even to this day, the alternate medication they chose sometimes failed to work also, and when this happened the fallback drug was always - you guessed it - chloral hydrate!

The week after I got settled, I contacted Dr. Richard Rowe at SickKids in Toronto, which was just an hour drive from Hamilton. I arranged to attend their cardio-surgical conference on Monday of each week. The commute always made for a fatiguing day regardless of whether I went by car or train. Dr. Rowe was kind enough to give me a cross appointment in cardiology and his entire team were supportive of my working at McMaster. Whenever I needed help with a case that appeared complex, or in need of surgery, they were always accommodating in making an appropriate assessment. They knew me well from my sabbatical time and welcomed my relocation to Hamilton.

The first Monday after my arrival I went to meet Dr. Rowe and attend the conference. He called me into his office and shut the door. He had some important news to share with me which would hit the press on the following Thursday. In the previous weeks, there had been several deaths on the cardiac unit resulting in a police investigation. All of the deaths appeared due to digoxin overdose, and a nurse was about to be arrested and charged with a criminal offense. By the time I returned on the following Monday the news was international and SickKids was in a state of crisis. Dr. Rowe briefed me again on what was known or suspected and, with his associate, Dr. Freedom, we had a private discussion on developments. The investigation continued over the next two years and was inconclusive with inadequate evidence to bring criminal charges against the individuals who were prime suspects. The problem disappeared but was never solved.

Meantime, back in Hamilton, my family got settled, and my professional work got under way. As expected, our older children felt cheated because they had been close to finishing High School in Newfoundland whereas now they were faced with doing extra years and completing grade thirteen. Some of the courses were repeats, which made school boring for them. Nevertheless, they persisted and graduated. Betty met with Susan's teachers to alert them to the areas where she might need some extra attention, and she did well subsequently. Our youngest, Steven, just beginning grade one, adjusted well without difficulty. Our oldest daughter, Caroline, encountered some bullying possibly because she was attractive and the other girls considered her as competition. Unfortunately, our home in St. John's did not sell for nearly nine months after the move. Then, we had a problem with the new owner taking possession before legal finalization of the sale. Eventually, things got settled and, by then, interest rates had fallen to more reasonable levels.

I worked at McMaster for nearly nineteen years before retirement. During that time, I enjoyed the support of some wonderful colleagues. Dr. Bill Wilson and I shared a secretary for practically all of my years there. One of our secretaries, Merry Green, was long serving and working with her was a real joy. When she came to her retirement, she decided she would help us find a replacement and arranged for Bill and me to interview a candidate. The candidate came one afternoon, and Bill led off the interview with some questions attempting to identify her secretarial skills. He was not very successful at obtaining any useful information, so my turn came to ask her some questions. We identified she was from Newfoundland and now did part time work in nearby Burlington. It was hard to identify what type of work she did but eventually she said she was feeling hot and took off her outer top. Then she appeared to get hotter and took off another layer. Finally, she was topless, and Bill and I were sitting speechless when the door opened and a camera flashed, and Merry and the entire office crew were standing there laughing at us two fools for having been duped. We had a good laugh, and everyone was a good sport. Naturally, we were the brunt of many jokes for the next week or so. After Merry's departure, our new secretary was Arlene, an excellent Christian lady who kept me on the straight and narrow for the rest of my career at McMaster.

I count it a privilege to have worked under two skilled chairpersons, Dr. Peter Dent and Dr. Jack Holland. Both were dedicated leaders and, although they had different styles, were very fair and understanding in dealing with issues. One of the major issues was the inadequate department funding that existed during their terms in office. I thought I had left insufficient funds behind in Newfoundland, but as soon as I arrived in Hamilton the economy slowed and the government largesse that fueled the development of health sciences at McMaster began to disappear. The lack of faculty funding resulted in geographic full-time (GFT) clinicians, like me, being expected to help pay their way by generating fee-for-service (FFS) money. The FFS money was collected and disbursed by Regional Medical Associates (RMA), a group practice plan set up to oversee payments to GFT clinicians. The faculty designed a system of remuneration known as 'Pay Code 4' whereby one's income was not paid in full if you did not generate sufficient FFS funds to cover your assigned costs PLUS the extra amount needed to cover the gap between base income (for academic work) and your ceiling. Consequently, many GFT physicians had to flog the fee-for-service system to make ends meet. In effect, we were paying the university for the privilege of teaching their medical students and working in their hospitals. Also, many clinicians, including me, had their ceiling froze for several years, a very detrimental situation to one's pension. This arrangement significantly disadvantaged the pediatric clinicians, as services to small patients were considered deserving of low fees compared to adult patient services. As a result, like many others, I became unhappy with income arrangements as retirement approached.

During my time at McMaster, we recruited a couple of associates in hope that they would assume leadership when I retired. The first associate we hired was a young woman who had trained at SickKids, and we worked well together for about five years. However, the pay issues were much in play at that time. She decided to leave us and enter private practice. I was alone again for a year or so and then we recruited a talented young man from the training programs in Edmonton and Calgary. He was well-trained and keen, with an interest in research. With his arrival, I was hopeful we had found the right candidate to lead the pediatric cardiology service on a long term basis. Unfortunately for us, after about five years, he was recruited to the staff of SickKids. After his departure, we were unable to hire a candidate considered suitable for the senior leadership role in pediatric cardiology. After I had retired, the staff expanded to four full-time physicians and at one point a lead physician was recruited from Germany, but he stayed only a few months.

My clinical work in Hamilton included the care of six patients who had received heart transplants for complex disease. During my first year, the surgical team at Loma Linda University in California was having great success with pediatric heart transplants, and we sent a 22-day old infant boy to them for an emergency procedure. He did exceptionally well and returned to us for long-term care after spending nearly the first two years of life in California. His family moved to Loma Linda for this time, and his father received employment for the duration of their stay. I should acknowledge the excellent work of Dr. Robyn Whyte, a colleague in the Neonatal Unit, who made the contacts with Loma Linda and worked out air transportation (Medevac) direct from Hamilton to the California Centre. When Timmy and his family returned to Hamilton, I had the challenging privilege of caring for him until he was nearly sixteen years old. I saw him and his mom for the last time when they came as guests to the retirement party, held by the Department of Pediatrics, to recognize my contributions over nineteen years at McMaster.

Following retirement as a full-time employee, I continued with clinical work at McMaster Children's Hospital for three years to assist with staffing needs in cardiology. After that I continued on a part-time basis for another seven years, filling in whenever needed, and finally retired in December 2009.

CHAPTER 28

Post Retirement Years

After retirement from academic duties, I continued with clinical work at McMaster Hospital for another ten years. The support and help of the Clinic staff during this additional time was much appreciated, and I thank the Pediatric Department leadership for permitting me to continue working. During the latter part of the ten years, I accepted some additional consultant work at the Cambridge Cardiology Clinic in Cambridge, and I continue to work there on a part-time basis (May 2016).

Our church life also changed shortly after retirement. When we arrived in Hamilton in early 1981, we were blessed by a warm welcome at West Highland Baptist Church. Soon after arriving, my wife and I were invited to join a prayer group that was partly from West Highland, to explore starting a church in Ancaster where we lived. After several months of prayer and planning, the group felt led to proceed, and Heritage Baptist Church began worship services in October. My wife and I, and family were actively involved in leadership, music, and youth activities at this new work for the next eight years and saw it expand and prosper. In the fall of 1989, after some leadership issues surfaced, we chose to return to West Highland, and Betty and I soon became involved in ministry roles there. Over the next fifteen years, I was active in leadership areas, including membership on pulpit search committees, as we worked through changes in pastoral leadership during that time.

As the year 2000 arrived West Highland Baptist Church was experiencing a dynamic pulpit ministry, attendance was edging towards 1000+ on Sunday mornings and dual services were started. Both Betty and I were involved in the choir and Betty was directing the drama program. The board, which included me, began serious discussions, and prayer, concerning how best to meet the ministry needs of an enlarging congregation. One obvious option was to enlarge the current building and architects were hired to design a church facility suitable for up to 2500 attendees. After several months, architect drawings arrived and were reviewed by the board and shared with the church membership for discussion and feedback. A second option, suggested by the local association of our denomination, was to start a daughter church in the east mountain area of Hamilton. Their president was a guest preacher at West Highland on at least two occasions and openly challenged the church to consider this option. I favored the latter idea but was not opposed to the concept of a larger building. My experience with churches over the years suggested that the ideal congregation size was around five hundred. Once a church reached that size, I felt, it was time to encourage some people to move out of the nest (comfortable pew) and move into another fertile field to savor the joy of spiritual reproduction.

While prayerfully examining these options, we were shocked by the resignation of our pastor. Discussions about building expansion ended. Nevertheless, over the next three years, even in the absence of a senior pastor there continued to be promptings to establish a daughter work and the interim church leadership expressed support for this. During this time, I was involved with the Pastoral Search Committee and finished my term on the board. Church attendance fell somewhat, as was expected, but the board was optimistic that this would recover once a new pastor came. After the new pastor arrived the focus became developing space for in-house growth and the idea of a daughter work was no longer encouraged. The church's long-standing space need was for Christian education and children's ministry, and this received immediate attention. As an initial step, the staff offices were moved to rented space in a nearby business complex and the basement was partially renovated to provide additional space for children's ministry.

In the meantime, Betty and I were exploring the option of moving house and downsizing. We loved living in Ancaster, but our nest was empty, and the town had more than doubled in the twenty-five years since our arrival. Traffic issues were a problem, and with incorporation into greater Hamilton it lost some of its focus on the role it played in Canadian history. By 2006, we were ready for a change and began exploring the surrounding area for an alternate location. Because of our interest in being part of a new church work on the east mountain we began to explore this area which had, in addition to large tracts of farmland, several small bedroom communities that were starting to grow.

Our research led us to Binbrook, a small town south of Stoney Creek, which was quickly growing beyond its farm crossroads status. It is close to the center of the east mountain and appealed to us as a fresh start for our retirement years. The need for a vibrant church work in the area was very evident. We found a quality builder for our home and a choice location in a new housing area close to the community's center. After a year of planning and watching our house built, we moved into a lovely new place which continues to delight us. After two more years, most of the survey's fifty-two homes were in place, the dust was settling, the pavement was down, and driveways were being completed. It took a couple more years to landscape the park on the back of our home, and the initial attempt had drainage problems but now, eight years later, it is lovely.

In the meantime, Binbrook changed from being just a center for farm business, at a crossroads with a traffic light. It became a booming and expanded community of fifteen thousand people with new schools, a post office, a library, senior citizens home, a fire hall, a theater, a Tim Horton's, two banks, a new shopping plaza, three drug stores, and several professional offices. The town outgrew its road system, water and sewage systems, and other infrastructure elements, all of which are receiving attention at this time. There are three small older churches in the community but, in our view, it is in need of a vibrant spiritual ministry to reach out to the young families flocking to this area. West Highland Baptist Church has a small group functioning in Binbrook, and we enjoy the fellowship of this group, but pray that one day a nucleus group will come together and feel led to oversee an attractive ministry on the east mountain of Hamilton. For about five years after our move, we attended a group in town that was designed to establish a daughter work out of Gateway Church in Caledonia. Unfortunately, we did not see progress in the group towards developing a foundation for a new church, so we decided to discontinue our association with them. In the meantime, we continue at West Highland, which we have been a part of for nearly thirty-five years. We enjoy the fellowship of our small group, the senior's ministry, and several men's ministry programs, and continue in several long time friendships there.

CHAPTER 29

Family Life

As I complete this record, Betty and I have celebrated 52 years of happy marriage. Our four children have grown to healthy adulthood without too much damage from having us as their parents. Neither of us went to a training school for parenting. Betty was fortunate to grow up in a stable home whereas my childhood experience was broken and traumatic.

To some extent we are creatures of our childhood experiences. I am well aware that during our early family years I was too busy professionally and otherwise to function properly as a parent. My children should have received greater attention from their father.

During my young adult years before marriage, I was focused on finding my way and obtaining a good education and career. After completing my training and moving back to Newfoundland, it took ten years to wake up and realize that there were more important things in life than medicine. By that time Gregory and Caroline were entering their adolescent years. The career moves I made, with a sabbatical and relocation, were not well-timed from their perspective as it fouled up their education schedule and experience. Nevertheless, we muddled through and maintained a cohesive relationship as a family.

I am particularly proud that our four children have kept close and supportive relationships as they have matured and moved out of the nest. It is wonderful too, to see the close relationships that are developing between our grandchildren as they grow. Betty and I are thankful for the resources provided to us to educate our children as well as lay aside a small endowment which, if needed, will help educate our grandchildren. Of course, it is my expectation

39. Family gathering, Thanksgiving 2010. Adults, Steven and Liz, Caroline, Susan and Ian, Cliff and Betty, Debbie and Gregory. Grandchildren, Sarah and Seth (Susan), Lucas and Thomas (Gregory), Eleanor and Veronica (Steven).

that our grandchildren will be much smarter than their grandparents, or parents, and will sail through higher education on scholarships!

Marriage and family life have been wonderful for me, in contrast to some of my experiences during childhood. During our years as a family in Newfoundland, we had lots of fun at church functions, visiting my relatives, doing picnics at Torbay, Cape Spear, and nearby Provincial Parks. Our summer trips to Lake Wallace, Quebec, to spend cottage time with friends and then to Montreal to visit Grandpa and Grandma Milne were always special times. While in Ancaster, we continued a close relationship with Betty's parents until they died. Grandpa Milne lived in Ancaster for his last five years, and we included him in all our family functions. As our children completed High School and higher education, we celebrated success with them. Three of our children married and have given us six grandchildren and we are thankful for all of that. Our oldest daughter spent six years in Virginia Beach attending University and recently published her first novel, and we have celebrated that. All of our children have had dogs as part of their family structure, and we have shared our love for animals with them.

We feel blessed by our family life and cherish the good memories.

CHAPTER 30
A well-traveled Way

TRAVEL HAS BEEN A SIGNIFICANT part of my life and career, so I felt it would be appropriate to call this autobiography *A well-traveled Way*. In a broader sense, my journey through life has a spiritual aspect to it as well. Every day, as I dealt with children with possible heart disease, and their anxious parents I became conscious of the fact that 'there but for the Grace of God go I'. From my childhood exposure and involvement in Christian things, I came to recognize that God had marked out a plan for me. As I look back, I realize that He did everything possible to provide people and circumstances along the way to protect, guide and care for me, even as I floundered and muddled through. My recognition of a higher power, or guardian angel, is not unique as countless others have recorded, down through the ages, God's timely provision and protection to them. I recognize too, as have many others, I have not been worthy of His favor and have not always followed His way. Nevertheless, He has never failed me but has blessed and prospered me in ways that would never have been possible without His gracious involvement. In a real sense, much of my life has been 'supernatural'. Yes indeed, it has been a well-traveled way.

CHAPTER 31

Final Thoughts And Commendation

When I started making this record, some twenty years ago, my motive was to provide a history for my children and grandchildren. I also realized, that since I grew up away from home after age thirteen, my relatives in Flower's Cove do not know, or have forgotten, many of the details I have recorded here. For my extended family, I am hoping this account will be a source of pride and thankfulness.

All of the Way family, but particularly Millie and I, are forever grateful for the precious love and care of our Grandmother Way, who provided for us in some of the darkest days of our childhood.

My sister would join me in making special mention of our Aunt Millie Kean and her sacrificial care for us during the same period.

There is an extensive list of people that God guided to help and care for me, and their family members should take pride in learning of their contributions to my success. I would specifically mention –

Rev. C. T. Mansfield, who opened the way for me to enter St. Anthony Orphanage and Grenfell School.

Dr. Gordon Thomas, who recruited financial help from Mrs. Charles Curtis to pay for my education at Sherbrooke High School and Bishop's University.

Dr. Arthur Hill, who served as my guardian during my time in Sherbrooke and at Bishop's.

Harold and Peggy Munkittrick, who 'adopted' me as their son during my teen years.

As you have read, the way was not all roses in my early years, but the Lord guided me through to an excellent education and directed my way into an enjoyable and satisfying career as a pediatric cardiologist. Above all, the Lord provided me with Betty, who has supported me faithfully through the tough and busy times. She has nurtured our four children and has been more responsible than I for raising them, and for giving us a happy family life together.

It is my hope; this record will again remind you of how God continues to work mysteriously and miraculously in the lives of many individuals to guide them along the way. Like Dr. Grenfell, Dr. Thomas, and many others who served at the Grenfell Mission, my experience confirms that following the call of Christ results in experiences that transcend anything available otherwise. It is the path to inner peace, and to assurance and hope for Life Eternal at the end of life's way. May you also be found in His way.

'Investigate my life, O God, Find out everything about me; Cross-examine and test me, get a clear picture of what I'm about; See for yourself whether I've done anything wrong – then guide me on the road to eternal life.'

[Psalm 139:23-24, The Message (MSG), Eugene H. Peterson]

APPENDIX 1

Abbreviated Way Family Tree

THE WAYS WERE ORIGINALLY FROM SW England. Fishermen in Bonavista, NL, in the 1700's.

1. **William Way,** born 1784) in Bonavista area. Wife, Mary Saint (b. 1788).
2. **John Way** (1805-1885), born Bonavista. Taught school and died at Little Catalina. Wife was Mary Templeton (1807-1893).
3. *****John Way (1829-1922),** born at Catalina. **Moved to Flower's Cove.** + First wife, Mary Coles.
4. **Sons of John Way and Mary Coles.**

Samuel (1852-1909), born Flower's Cove. Moved to Harrington Hr., Labrador. Wife, Caroline Penney (1852-1909).
John (b 1854), born Flower's Cove. Moved to Savage Cove.
Benjamin (1866-1929), Born and lived in Flower's Cove.
George (1861-1929) + Moriah Moores (b 1871). Born and lived in Flower's Cove. Parents of Abraham, Sisley ('Sis'), Beatrice, Delilah. Builder of my childhood home.
Henry "Harry" (1857-1932) + Susanna Norman ("Gam") (1866-1951).

5. **Sons of "Harry Way" and Susanna Norman.**

-**Henry William Antle** (1890-1935) + Delilah Way (1895-1935). Children – Maryanne (b 1918) and Grenfell (Grant) (1926-2015).
-**Augustus "Gus" Way** (1888-1964) + Susanna Genge (1896-1983). [My Grandparents]

6. **Children of Augustus Way and Susanna Genge.**

-Johanna (1913-1999) + Rex Penney. (Eastport, Bonavista Bay, NL)
- Stewart Way (1915-1976) + Hazel Coles (1923-2006).
-**Aubrey George (1916-1945)** + Caroline Kean (b 1912). **My Parents.**
-Lavenia Pearl (1917-1944) + Nelson Coles. (Savage Cove, NL)
- Leander Percy (Pierce) (1920-1985) + Mary Lawless (1918-1998).
-Abraham (1922-2006) + Rosalind Rose. (1927-2014) (Flower's Cove)
-Ella, born Feb 07, 1925. Died Sept. 30, 1925.
- Israel Maxwell (1923- 2004) + Mabel Genge (1921-2009).
-Alma (1928-) + Lester Penney. (St. Anthony, NL)
-Henry (1930 - 2003) + (1) Dora Coles. (2) Sadie Noseworthy.
-Bertha Jane (1931-) + Montrose Genge. (Flower's Cove, NL)
-Clayton, born April 20, 1934. Died June 20, 1934.

7. **Children of Aubrey George Way and Caroline Kean.**

-**Roland Clifton Kean**, born April 10, 1934, + Betty Margaret Forsyth Milne. Children of Roland Clifton Kean Way and Betty Margaret Milne.

David **Gregory**, born March 25, 1965, at St. Anthony. Married Debbie Bennett. Children, Thomas (2000), Lucas (2002).

Caroline Margaret, born July 6, 1966, in Portland, Oregon, USA.

Susan Elizabeth (1969) at St. John's, NL. Married Ian McKeeman. Children– Sarah (1997) and Seth (2003)

Steven Clifton (1975) at St. John's, NL. Married Elizabeth Kalbfleish. Children–Eleanor (2005),Veronica (2008)

-**Baxter**, born 1936. Died 1938.

-**Amelia Adelphia**, (1939) + Willie P. Simms. Married November 1964.

Children – Nadine, Deanne, Lisa, Gordon.

***3. John Way (1829-1922)**) + second wife Annie Adams, were Parents of **Arabella** (1879-1975) and **Rachel** (1883-1971). Arabella married Alfred Cowan (Nova Scotia) and had a large number of descendants there. Rachel married John Rose, Flower's Cove, and was childless but raised Wilson and Duke Moores as foster children after their parents died of tuberculosis.

APPENDIX 2

Abbreviated Kean Family Tree

1. William Kean, Born 1633, Teignmouth, Exeter, England.
2. William Kean (1658-1730). Born in Salem, Mass. Died at Concord, Mass.
3. William Kean (1712-1775). Returned to Teignmouth and died there.
4. William Kean (1739-1786) + Mary Carter (Born 1751)
5. Samuel Kean (1772-1822) + Mary Rule (1778-1852).
6. William Kean (1810-1887) + Ann Janes. (William one of seven children).

William's brother, Joseph, (1814-1883) was the father of Capt. Abram Kean (1855-1945), famous sealing captain and politician in Newfoundland.

7. Benjamin Kean (1838-1906) + Marion Spurrell (1838-1913). (Benjamin one of 15 children).
8. Eleazer Kean (1865-1952) + Caroline Sheppard. (Eleazer one of 11 children).
9. **Harold Clifton Roland Kean (1888-1969) + Amelia Genge (1891-1930) (1).**
    +Julia Genge (1899-1943) (**2**). + Gladys Coombs (3).

10. Children of H. C. 'Roland' Kean and Amelia Genge.
    10. Cecil Kean (b 1910) + May Peckford. (Plum Point, NL)
    10. ***Caroline Kean (b 1912)** + *Aubrey Way. (**My** parents)
    10. Stella Kean (b 1914) + Caleb Whalen. (Flower's Cove, NL)
    10. Marjorie Kean (b 1917) + Lorenzo Whalen. (Flower's Cove, NL)
    10. Selina Kean (b 1919) + Eldon Hedge. (Corner Brook, NL)
    10. **Amelia Kean**. (Mother of 'little' Marjorie Kean). My stepmother.

Children of H. C. 'Roland' Kean and Julia Genge.
    10. Annie Kean (**2**) + Gerald McHugh. (Corner Brook, NL)
    10. Marion Kean (**2**) + Dave Cook. (South Glovertown, NL)
    10. Weston Kean (**2**). Died at age 14.

APPENDIX 3

Abbreviated Family Tree Of Genge Families

A. GENGES OF DEADMAN'S COVE (Grandmother Kean's family).

2. *****William Genge (1) (a relative of an original settler at Anchor Point)** + daughter of William Buckle and a Watts girl. The Watts girl was from Labrador. Her father was from Scotland, and her mother was a Labrador native.
   Son of William Genge (1) and daughter of William Buckle.
3. ******William Genge (2)**. He had three wives.
   +Joanna Duncan (**1st wife**)
   +Susanna Whelan (**2nd wife**) from Flower's Cove.
   +Elizabeth (Brown) Williams (**3rd wife**)
4. **Isaac Henry Genge****, born 1859 at Anchor Point). Son of William Genge and **2nd wife**. Married Margaret Godfrey (born 1861) from Forteau, Labrador. They settled at Deadman's Cove.

Children of Isaac Henry Genge** and Margaret Godfrey.
   (2)Angus (b 1883) + Minnie Chambers (Bear Cove). Lived in Flower's Cove.
   (2)Isaac (b 1901) He and his family lived in Flower's Cove.

175

(2)Charles (b 1895) + Eva (b 1897) He and his family lived in Deadman's Cove.

(2)Margaret (b 1906). Married Martin Bugden of Norris Point, Bonne Bay.

(2)James. He and his family lived at Deadman's Cove.

(2)Lambert. He and his family lived at Deadman's Cove.

(2)Abraham. Moved to Clearwater, Florida.

(2)**Amelia Genge** (1890-1930) + **Harold Clifton Roland Kean** (1888-1969). (My maternal grandparents). Six children, including my mother, **Caroline**.

(3)**Caroline Kean (1912-1941) + Aubrey George Way (1916-1945). (My parents.)**

B. GENGES OF ANCHOR POINT. (Grandmother Way's family). First two generations same as above –

1. *****William Genge (1)** (a relative of an original settler at Anchor Point) + daughter of William Buckle and his wife who was a Watts girl from Labrador. Her father, known only as Mr. Watts, was from Scotland, and her mother was a Labrador native.
Son of William Genge (1) and Ms. Buckle.

2. ******William Genge (2)**. He had three wives.
+Joanna Duncan (**1st wife**) (Surname 'Duncan' later became 'Gould') Probably from Bear Cove, which is just north of Anchor Point.
+Susanna Whelan (**2nd wife**) from Flower's Cove.
+Elizabeth (Brown) Williams (**3rd wife**). Unsure of maiden name and origin.

3. *******Israel Genge,** born 1872, was the son of **William Genge (2) and 3rd wife.** He Married Bridget Gould in 1895.

One of their daughters was Susannah Genge (1895-1981).
Susannah married Augustus Way, March 26, 1913. She was my father's mother.

Isaac Henry Genge, my Grandmother Kean's dad, was the half-brother of **Israel Genge,** my Grandmother Way's dad. A full brother, William (3), was the father of Henry Genge, owner of the store in Flower's Cove where my parents worked before marriage.

William Genge (1) was a son of the brother (name not recorded) of Abram Genge. Abram was a nephew of William Bartlett, the original settler in Anchor Point. (For additional details see book by Irving Letto, **'Sealskin Boots and a Printing Press,'** *Piecing together the life of Canon J. T. Richards*, pages 158-162, Produced by Friesen Press, November 2012.)

APPENDIX 4

Abbreviated Milne Family Tree

(Family of my wife, Betty Milne)
1. John Milne (born 1650), Mill of Andlethen, near Aberdeen, Scotland.
2. George Milne (born 1678), Mains of Esslemont. Married Elizabeth Temple.
3. Alexander Milne (1734-1830) + Margaret Sangster.
4. Alexander Milne (1775-1871) + Anne Jamieson (1792-1874).
5. Alexander Milne (1817-1902) + Christian Garden. Scotland.
6. Alexander Milne (1844-1936) +Helen Hay Walker (died 1911). Scotland.
7. **Alexander Milne** (1871-1943) + Agnes Forsyth (1869-1953). Immigrated to Canada (Montreal), 1912.
8. **George Walker Milne** (1904 – 2002) + **Jessie Williamson**. George was one of seven children.

Children of George Walker Milne and Jessie Williamson.

9. George Alexander Craig Milne + Gerda Hempel. (Betty's brother and wife in Regina, Saskatchewan.)
10. *****Betty Margaret Forsyth Milne** + **Roland Clifton Kean Way.**

Acknowledgements

1. Audrey Dorsch for her professional editing and advice.
2. Rev. A. Morris Russell for his helpful review and input.
3. Rev. Dr. Grant Gordon for his detailed review of the manuscript.
4. Mr. Steve Oswald for his review and editorial input.

Author Biography

R. Clifton "Cliff" Way, MD, FRCPC, FACC, was born in Flower's Cove, a small outport in northern Newfoundland. At seven, he lost his mother to tuberculosis. His father died when Cliff was eleven, and the young boy went to live with his grandparents.

He began his education in a one-room schoolhouse but went on to graduate from Bishop's University in 1953. After a year working in a paper mill, he was admitted to McGill University's medical school, graduating in 1958.

Way completed his postgraduate training at hospitals in Quebec, British Columbia, and Oregon. He was a staff member and acting chief of medicine at the Janeway Child Health Center. In 1981 he became the first director of pediatric cardiology at McMaster University, Hamilton, where he practiced and taught until retirement.

Cliff and his wife, Betty, live in Binbrook, Ontario. They have four children and six grandchildren, all of whom live nearby.

CPSIA information can be obtained
at www.ICGtesting.com
Printed in the USA
LVHW081537030419
612832LV00031B/648/P